DO NOT DL...

Without Presidential Approval

WES ANDERSON was born in Houston, Texas. His films include *Bottle Rocket, Rushmore, The Royal Tenenbaums, The Life Aquatic with Steve Zissou, The Darjeeling Limited, Fantastic Mr. Fox, Moonrise Kingdom, The Grand Budapest Hotel, Isle of Dogs,* and *The French Dispatch.* His latest film is *Asteroid City.*

JACOB "JAKE" PERLIN is a film programmer, distributor and publisher. He is the founding Artistic Director of Metrograph. His companies, The Film Desk and Film Desk Books, recently released *Vengeance is Mine* (Michael Roemer, 1984) and *No Fear No Die* (Claire Denis, 1990), and new editions of *Film as a Subversive Art* by Amos Vogel and *Diary of a Film* by Jean Cocteau. Perlin also oversees Cinema Conservancy, a non-profit whose most recent release is *James Baldwin: From Another Place* (Sedat Pakay, 1973). He was named Chevalier de l'Ordre des Arts et des Lettres and received a special award from the New York Film Critics Circle for his "Indispensable contributions to film culture."

DO NOT DETONATE
Without Presidential Approval

A Portfolio on the Subjects of
MID-CENTURY CINEMA
the **BROADWAY STAGE**
and the
AMERICAN WEST

Inspirations for **Wes Anderson's**
ASTEROID CITY
Edited by Jake Perlin

PUSHKIN PRESS

Pushkin Press
Somerset House, Strand
London WC2R 1LA

DO NOT DETONATE was first published by Pushkin Press in 2023

All texts reprinted faithfully from original publication.

3 5 7 9 8 6 4 2

ISBN 13: 978-1-80533-051-6

Designed and typeset by Tetragon, London

Printed and bound by Clays Ltd, Elcograf S.p.A.

www.pushkinpress.com

CONTENTS

IN THE ORBIT OF
ASTEROID CITY

A Conversation Between Wes Anderson and Jake Perlin

JAKE: When beginning to discuss this collection, we knew that it would take a different direction than books that accompanied *The Grand Budapest Hotel* and *The French Dispatch*. For *The Society of the Crossed Keys*, all the writing was by Stefan Zweig, and for *An Editor's Burial*, for the most part, David Brendel selected pieces or found original correspondence that illuminated the history of *The New Yorker*, or were the very specific references for that film.

WES: This one is more about the atmosphere of it. With *The French Dispatch*, it was made of fictionalized works of journalism based on specific voices that we're trying to kind of channel. With this one, that's not remotely the case. This one has some broad inspirations, but it doesn't have direct sources the way *The French Dispatch* did.

JAKE: Right. And you take it further in *The French Dispatch*, too, with Frances McDormand's Mavis Gallant character.

WES: I mean, we quote her.

JAKE: You actually quoted her.

WES: Repeatedly. There are four or five lines that are just direct quotations from her *Paris Notebooks*. We even went to her estate and said, "Look, we want to quote these." And, it's funny, the reaction was simply and completely: "We have no legal right to authorize or not. You don't need our permission. Those quotes fall under 'fair use.'"

JAKE: That's the ideal response from an estate.

WES: On a legal basis, the ideal response. Perhaps one hopes for a bit more, such as: "How interesting! What are you doing? Is there anything more you want from us?" What we got was: "That's 'fair use.' You don't need to be in touch with us." Which works, too.

JAKE: There were characters in past films who are direct inspirations, but here it's elements that might read as one person, like Scarlett Johansson as Monroe, perhaps another, or a combination.

WES: Yes. I mean, for instance, that character, we think of Marilyn Monroe first. She was a movie star who sort of aspired to be more like the great actors of the stage, and her relationship with The Actors Studio became a part of The Actors Studio, itself; but it was also sort of aspirational for her, and it becomes this sort of power dynamic with Paula Strasberg. There's a lore around it. There's Arthur Miller and *The Misfits*. That brings us out West. It's the tie to New York City. It's a room in Gramercy Park, but it's also a herd of wild horses. What do you call a pack of horses? A herd. Anyway, there they are. We're in the desert, and it swirls together a number of those things. But also with that character, I think a bit about Kim Stanley, mostly a stage actress. There's one movie that's called *The Goddess*. That's the one where she plays a movie star, and it sort of refers to herself, I guess. Jane Russell also is another. The costumes are Grace Kelly and Kim Novak. There's a costume taken straight from *Rear Window*, and there's another from *Vertigo*. It's a swirl of characters with a lot of Marilyn Monroe. I think even though our character talks about being the person you find on the floor of the bathroom with an empty bottle of sleeping pills, the person who actually *says* that is different, if you see what I mean, from the one who does it.

JAKE: That makes sense. That's what led me to use the Eve Arnold photographs from the set of *The Misfits*, of course, but when looking at the dozens of images of her work there were particular ones that really seemed to match up with *Asteroid City*. This was not something we had discussed previously, and I assume that was not intentional on your part to be so specific in duplicating any of Eve Arnold's work, however well you may know it. But there it is, a picture of Monroe on the set with a young girl, much like the mother–daughter relationship in the film, or both wearing robes. But these connections were made after seeing the film and looking at more of the photos than I had initially had in mind, my memory of the photos. That was much of the fun of this, discovering things I think neither of us had considered, like a parallel film.

WES: I don't know if I mentioned this, but Eve Arnold was very good friends with my wife Juman's mother. There is a shot of Clark Gable running in Nevada right across the room from me. Which does not belong to me. It belongs to them, but I've taken it and put it in here. By the way, have you ever seen one I saw recently, Sidney Lumet's *Stage Struck*? Susan Strasberg. It's her big role. I mean, she's in *Picnic*, but those were kind of her biggest.

JAKE: *Diary of Anne Frank*, on stage.

WES: Yes! Only on the stage. And I think those are her biggest things. This is with Henry Fonda, and I would connect our character to this one if I had seen that before we made *Asteroid City*, but I didn't.

JAKE: Right. Well, the way that also connects is we found an amazing photograph by Roy Schatt of Monroe and Susan Strasberg, and the piece by Lillian Ross visiting Strasberg at home. And though you hadn't mentioned *Stage Struck*, you had mentioned *12 Angry Men*, and we have another Roy Schatt photograph of Lumet directing live television with Lorne Greene. I mean Lorne Greene's back is to the camera but we'll take his word for it, and in the photo Lumet is an absolute dead ringer for Adrien Brody in *Asteroid City*.

WES: Roy Schatt did a lot of pictures of James Dean, right? There's Dennis Stock and Roy Schatt.

JAKE: Roy Schatt did the series with Dean that he calls the torn sweater series.

WES: Which we steal directly from, too.

JAKE: There is a shot of Jason with his feet up just like Dean wearing Converse Jack Purcells.

WES: And with his sweater pulled up over his nose. That's from that series of photographs.

JAKE: The first logline for the film that came out was: "Desert Town, 1950, Junior Stargazers." That was all I knew going into the film other than it had been shot in Spain. But everything that surrounds that, particularly having to do with The Actors Studio, takes up as much of the film and really gives us the structure. Were they always going to be part of the same film?

WES: I wanted to do a theater movie, a movie about the 1950s. I was thinking of it like Paul Newman and Joanne Woodward. Something that sort of goes from summer stock and then into the city and gives us a 1950s Broadway story. Paul Newman in a T-shirt in The Actors Studio.

JAKE: Yes, sitting on the backwards chair, by Eve Arnold. Worth noting this image is in the book, but this is the first time we are discussing it.

WES: Yes. So that was part of the beginning of it. And we had an idea of doing a making-of-the-play that they're working on. But at that point, the play we were calling "Automat," and it was going to be set entirely in an automat, and that was going to be the play. At the same time, the other thing that we, Roman and me, were sort of talking about was something kind of Sam Shepard. I love Sam Shepard, I've always loved Sam Shepard. Owen and I were really quite fixated on Sam Shepard before we made our first movie together. This guy was a big part of our lives at that time. I remember reading something about him talking about these men who had come back from the Second World War, and they were never the same, these violent and disturbed fathers. What he grew up with. These men who end up out somewhere near Needles or something. I remember him talking in one interview about how his father actually went to see one of the plays in a production somewhere out in California, in Fresno, I don't know where he was, and made a scene. Shouting at the actors. He died, hit by a car, I think trying to get his dog out of the highway in front of a bar.

JAKE: That's kind of like *Wild to the Wild*, with the dog on the tracks...

WES: The dog just leaves, in the end, doesn't it?

JAKE: Yes, they're worried about it getting killed on the tracks. They're trying to get it off the tracks.

WES: So we shifted out of "Automat" and into the desert. But I do always feel that a movie for me is not one idea. It's sort of at least two sort of separate things that come together and start to become a movie.

JAKE: Right. In the interview with Susan Morrison for *An Editor's Burial*, you mentioned something similar that Tom Stoppard had said.

WES: Exactly.

JAKE: I think this film takes that many steps further. It seems the ultimate of that idea. It's hard for me on one viewing to decide what the primary story is. The opening is from the booth of a live television studio, a *Playhouse 90* type studio. From the beginning you're not where you expect to be.

WES: Yes. "Am I seeing the right movie? I thought it's in the desert."

JAKE: We have this piece from *Time* magazine from 1957 about *Playhouse 90*, a great piece on the set of *Playhouse 90* when Frankenheimer was directing an episode with Ben Gazzara. It's just a report from that moment in time.

WES: I love it.

JAKE: I am hoping some of the pieces in the book set the background a bit, I wouldn't want this to be my asking, "Oh, is that Frankenheimer?" because different characters are amalgams but it's all a creation on your and Roman's part.

WES: I'm happy to talk about where they come from, because to me, part of the movie is a bit of a little conversation about some things that we're interested in sort of historically, and that has a lot to do with the New York stage, and also Hollywood, and so on. At the same time I have the slightest reluctance to make it too much about that aspect of it and to not go somehow into what is this movie actually about? And who these people actually are? Who are these characters aside from who they refer to or who inspired them? Ultimately, I hope somebody has an experience watching the movie where all this stuff that swirls around it is interesting, and enhances it, and informs it. But hopefully the thing itself, the kind of movie it is, we're aiming for something a bit more in the vein of a poem. That's sort of our goal. A poetic meditation on something or other. There certainly isn't a genre that we can put it in.

JAKE: It all exists in the same orbit as the film, in the spirit of, as you said. All the new writing in the book makes no reference to *Asteroid City* at all, it all stands independently as criticism, as you wanted. Just that these are films you had said played some role in the conception of the film, but not explaining further than that allows us to find texts and images that illuminate the period, but not being direct references.

WES: What's underneath it? When you set a movie in this time: what's the America that we're trying to write about?

What emotionally is underneath The Actors Studio? What's happening to them? Obviously The Actors Studio is a very political theater, a political group, and what happens to these people? Something not very good over the next decade and a half. Things get quite wild in America, at least some of the leadership of America brings this to them. And then also looking at someone like, for instance, Marilyn Monroe to see how this world of people end up and how they get there. Anyway, all of that somehow I feel, was feeding into this. And for me, it's a reason why, when I started wanting to make movies, this period was the center of everything. We were watching *The Godfather* and *Taxi Driver* and Brian De Palma. But, maybe even more: Marlon Brando and James Dean, Montgomery Clift and Kazan. The emotion of this period of movies and their relationship to the stage. This block of movies I'm talking about which maybe sort of begins with *Streetcar*. Tennessee Williams is a big voice of this urgency and the wounded whatever-it-is of these characters. I remember reading Marlon Brando described in the *World Book Encyclopedia* in kind of very masculine terms, like a boxer, but it also referred to him having a, quote, poetic face. There's something in that I think is interesting.

JAKE: Brando is the most revolutionary thing that happens to performance in the modern era.

WES: And maybe Brando himself only exists with all the combinations of things going on around him. You know, some kind of proto-beatnik or something at that point. And he's definitely going to be different from the people around him.

On the farm. But, you know, Brando without Kazan, I don't know. You have to have Gadge.

JAKE: This is all happening under a political cloud of the end of the war, paranoia around communism, atomic testing…

WES: The thing they're doing, to some degree, they're thinking of it as Russian. We know this is where they are looking.

JAKE: Going back to the Group Theatre days…

WES: …and they're becoming communists and then that's leading to the wildest turmoil and yet somehow the distance between being an actor on stage and a hydrogen bomb is not so far. It's a very peculiar era and so anyway we seemed to try to put some of it in there. A backdrop of paranoia. I don't know how often people use a nuclear detonation as a leitmotif.

JAKE: Yeah, there is a sense of dread that hangs over everything in that period, including the actors. Over all those actors. Going back to Kazan, he is really the person that carries the New York stage to Hollywood, I should say most successfully because Odets was there first, but by taking Brando or Clift or Dean or Monroe along with him, all the people that sort of defined the screen in the late fifties and into the early sixties. Poitier, Paul Newman, and Joanne Woodward are people that were at The Actors Studio. But there is also Tennessee Williams, he seems as crucial a person in this development as anyone.

WES: Our playwright is some mixture of the writers from this period. William Inge and Arthur Miller. But somehow emotionally underneath it, I guess the one that sort of moves us the most is Tennessee Williams, even if our play is not a great Tennessee Williams sort of play. We ended up putting him living in something like Truman Capote's house in Montauk. It does all sort of swirl together.

JAKE: So you've seen the Maysles Brothers' film *With Love from Truman*?

WES: Yes!

JAKE: When they go out and shoot him in Montauk in winter?

WES: Yes. Owen and I, it must have been just before or after we made *Rushmore*, I somehow got in touch with the Maysles. I wanted to see some of the films, and one in particular I wanted to see was *Meet Marlon Brando*, and the films weren't out there at that time.

JAKE: *With Love from Truman*, *Meet Marlon Brando*, and the total masterpiece *Showman*, about Joseph Levine.

WES: And the Beatles. Somehow we arranged to go over to where they were in those days. It was before they moved uptown. They were in midtown. We went there and they put us into a sort of closet, and we went two days in a row and watched one Maysles film after another. They had a bunch of kids in there, in a great big studio workplace for people, and it was such a great kind of thing to do in New York, to manage to talk your way in.

JAKE: There are clear references to Spielberg in *Asteroid City*— and also a familiar, warm feeling, so recognizable, of kids outwitting adults, a military mobilization...

WES: Yes, maybe our quarantine comes partly from real life, where the whole planet was in it; but, yes, maybe almost as much comes from *Close Encounters*, especially being in quarantine under false pretenses.

JAKE: There's an element of Spielberg's "Watch the Skies" films, naturally, with the Junior Stargazer Convention...

WES: I think some of that got brainwashed into me. I wasn't deliberately trying to do something Spielbergy; but he has so much to do with me waiting in line on Saturday afternoons for three hours to pay $4 for a ticket. All those years. All those two-hour blocks of life.

JAKE: I know you had Kubrick in mind. But Kubrick himself, his myth or style, perhaps?

WES: I think Jason maybe thought of Kubrick's speaking voice and what he looked like and his funny mystique. Yes, Kubrick and Spielberg. *2001* is this austere, giant sort of art movie. Maybe the biggest art movie ever made? He tells us a story, but he gives us an experience we don't necessarily understand every step of the way. He's puts us in a place where we have never even remotely been. By the time of *Close Encounters*, Spielberg had already found one of his own totally unique movie-making voices—his Amblin voice, if that sounds right—and *that* is a place where we have never been (though everything in it is especially familiar).

JAKE: You mentioned *Nashville* in connection to *Asteroid City*—is that film more of an eternal reference for your work?

WES: *Nashville* is some kind of musing about America at that moment. You know, it's a free association about the country. It's also one of those movies where there's lots of different characters who are all interacting and coming and going around an event, and they've all come into one place together. So I guess it's for those reasons that I bring it up. Beyond that, I don't really know. The thing I always love about Altman, but *Nashville* in particular, is how he has this approach of getting these ingredients, and he's seeing what happens to this, maybe add a little something here and push it around there, and then see what happens and what can this person do. And yeah, some of that's good and some of that's not so good. We'll throw some of that into the mix, too. And it's almost like cooking, his way was really like a bit of a kitchen. Now you guys go write a song and let me hear it and see what you can do. And you go away over here and you guys figure out what's the story between the two of you. I don't know what happened between the two of you. Maybe you guys will sort that out and then come back and tell me. And I felt a bit of that during the making of this movie because we had such a big cast and they would do things on their own. The way these kids worked together was very much in line with that. They were becoming their own little unit. And I like that. They've grown this together. So I think about Altman, in a way, as relating to the process. In *M*A*S*H*, there's something else that is heavier that's in the mix, too. And it's sort of not really what's played, but it's there. *Nashville* ends with an assassination and, you know, *M*A*S*H* every now and then there's blood all over everybody.

JAKE: The surgery is very graphic. Pauline Kael, famously and controversially, wrote her rave of *Nashville* after watching an unfinished cut.

WES: Did she do it because she said to Altman, "Let me write the rave before anybody else has even seen the movie—so it can do its most good"?

JAKE: She had a lot of pride in wanting to see her guys succeed, like Altman and De Palma and Schrader. At that moment, Altman needed a boost. Kael compared the premiere of *Last Tango in Paris* to the premiere of *Rite of Spring*. She makes grand pronouncements, and realizes they can benefit the filmmaker. I think that's a purpose of the review, and it's a scoop.

WES: Her piece about *Bonnie and Clyde*, I suppose, that one came late and made a big difference. But here, instead to give it a boost at the beginning. *Bonnie and Clyde*, what's sort of radical about it doesn't change the fact that it's a genre-type movie. And *Nashville*, you couldn't say that about it. I don't know what movie *Nashville* is. I can't imagine that *Nashville* was a big hit.

JAKE: I think in that case, yes, she felt it could do the most good. How big of a hit it was I don't know, but it did well, and it's as defining a film as you get in the mid-seventies.

WES: Exactly. The thing with Kael is part of her angle is to go to stick pins into the balloon, and it's not anti-intellectual, that isn't really the right description, but she's so anti-pretension that it almost becomes she's against the intellectuals who will voice their opinions in language that she finds pretentious. And that's such a big part of her voice, the voice she finds to express her feelings about movies, like it's a conversation and it's direct and it's what you say when you walk out the theater with your mind racing in one direction or another. She loved Godard. She wrote great pieces about Bellocchio and she's kind of a little bit anti-Fellini at moments. And she loved *L'Avventura*, which you could just as easily see her loathing. In her review of *Casualties of War*, when she talks about the greatest movies, the movies are *Grand Illusion* and *Shoeshine*, although oddly, it's *Grand Illusion*, *Shoeshine* and *The Chant of Jimmie Blacksmith*, which is a good Fred Schepisi movie, but it's probably not *Grand Illusion*.

JAKE: That is true. It was an art-house hit at the time, though.

WES: It's subjective. It's her field. It's her. And she loved Schepisi and she wrote about one Schepisi film after another. An interesting one we may not have seen lately. Is it called *Iceman*? With Timothy Hutton and John Lone. There are some good Schepisi movies. *Six Degrees of Separation* also is a really good one, but I think *Iceman*. I bet that's good. I probably haven't seen that movie in thirty years or something. I'm going to order it on Blu-ray right now.

A LIFE

EXCERPT

Elia Kazan

T HERE WAS ONE EXCEPTION to all my downgrading,
and when the dinner bell clanged, I watched him walk
down the hill from the cottage above—the living quarters,
I'd gathered, of the camp's elite. Descending like Zeus from
Olympus, the other man who'd interviewed me on the top
floor of the Forty-eighth Street Theatre didn't greet those he
passed. The camp had made him not more ordinary but more
exceptional. He was accompanied by his mistress, priestess
to his worship. He seemed anything but anxious about her,
walked a little ahead as they strolled toward the dining hall
at a pace he set. Apparently Lee Strasberg was still involved
in what he'd been studying when the dinner bell had interrupted his work.

In the next few days I was to discover that this unyielding
remoteness was habitual with Lee. He carried with him the
aura of a prophet, a magician, a witch doctor, a psychoanalyst,
and a feared father of a Jewish home. He was the center of the
camp's activities that summer, the core of the vortex. Everything
in camp revolved around him. Preparing to direct the play
that was to open the coming season, as he had the three plays

of the season before, he would also give the basic instruction in acting, laying down the principles of the art by which the Group worked, the guides to their artistic training. He was the force that held the thirty-odd members of the theater together, made them "permanent." He did this not only by his superior knowledge but by the threat of his anger.

On the morning of December 7, 1941, when Pearl Harbor was sneak-bombed by the Japanese, Admiral Ernest King was quoted: "Well, they've got themselves into a war. Now they need a son of a bitch to fight it." He was speaking of his government and meant himself. Sometimes only a tough, unyielding man can do a job that's for the good of all. Admiral King was necessary after Pearl Harbor, and Lee Strasberg was necessary that summer in 1933. He enjoyed his eminence just as the admiral would. Actors are as self-favoring as the rest of humanity, and perhaps the only way they could be held together to do their work properly was by the threat of an authority they respected. And feared.

Clearly Lee thought so. He had a gift for anger and a taste for the power it brought him. No one questioned his dominance—he spoke holy writ—his leading role in that summer's activities, and his right to all power. To win his favor became everyone's goal. His explosions of temper maintained the discipline of this camp of high-strung people. I came to believe that without their fear of this man, the Group would fly apart, everyone going in different directions instead of to where he was pointing.

I was afraid of him too. Even as I admired him.

Lee was making an artistic revolution and knew it. An

organization such as the Group—then in its second year, which is to say still beginning, still being shaped—lives only by the will of a fanatic and the drive with which he propels his vision. He has to be unswerving, uncompromising, and unadjustable. Lee knew this. He'd studied other revolutions, political and artistic. He knew what was needed, and he was fired up by his mission and its importance.

.   .   .   .   .

The next day, Lee put the Group people to work: the classes in the art of acting. Everything he taught was opposite to the instructions I'd listened to at Yale. Two young actresses, apprentices as I was, did a scene. When they were through, they looked to him for judgment. He said nothing. They waited. He stared at them. His face gave no hint of what he thought, but it was forbidding. The two actresses began to come apart; everyone could see they were on the verge of tears. Silence is the cruelest weapon when someone loves you, and Lee knew it. Finally one of them, in a voice that quavered, asked, "Lee, what did you think?" He turned his face away, looked at the other actors present. No one dared comment for fear of saying the wrong thing and having Lee turn on them. Finally, speaking quietly, he asked the stricken actress, "Are you nervous and uncertain now?" "Yes, yes," one actress said. "More than you were in the scene you played?" Lee asked. "Yes." "Much more?" "Yes, much more." "Even though the scene you did was precisely about such nervousness and you'd worked hard to imitate it?" "Oh, I see, I see," the actress said, getting Lee's point that now they were experiencing the real emotion whereas before they'd been pretending. He wanted the real emotion, insisted on the "agitation of the essence," as it was called, wouldn't accept less.

At his classes in the technique of acting, Lee laid down the rules, supervised the first exercises. These were largely concerned with the actor's arousing his inner temperament. The essential and rather simple technique, which has since then been complicated by teachers of acting who seek to make the Method more recondite for their commercial advantage, consists of recalling the circumstances, physical and personal, surrounding an intensely emotional experience in the actor's past. It is the same as when we accidentally hear a tune we may have heard at a stormy or an ecstatic moment in our lives, and find, to our surprise, that we are reexperiencing the emotion we felt then, feeling ecstasy again or rage and the impulse to kill. The actor becomes aware that he has emotional resources; that he can awaken, by this self-stimulation, a great number of very intense feelings; and that these emotions are the materials of his art.

Lee taught his actors to launch their work on every scene by taking a minute to remember the details surrounding the emotional experience in their lives that would correspond to the emotion of the scene they were about to play. "Take a minute!" became the watchword of that summer, the phrase heard most often, just as this particular kind of inner concentration became the trademark of Lee's own work when he directed a production. His actors often appeared to be in a state of self-hypnosis. When he directed a love scene, the "lovers" would seem to be not altogether aware of whom they were with but, instead, involved with their own inner state. There'd be no hint of how they proposed to consummate their love.

When Harold* began, three years later, to direct the company Lee had trained, he had some difficulties. Once, when asked repeatedly by an actor what the motivation in a love scene was, Harold is said to have burst out with: "Why, you want to fuck her, that's your motivation." Harold was a complicated man, but he didn't choose to make things more complicated than they were.

During the summer of 1932, I completely subscribed to Lee's method. I used to collect my useful memories in a notebook, tabulating these experiences so I could look through them, as through a file, and find the emotion a scene needed and how to awaken it. This collection was called "The Golden Box," and I still have the notebook, with my store of emotions in it.

After an actor had played a scene, Lee would ask, "What were you trying to do?" Immediately the actor found himself on the defensive, with an explanation demanded. The judge at this trial was sometimes a "hanging judge." There was little joy in Lee's work—only guilt for the deviants and a kind of psychological restriction, which made a wild fling into experiment, humor, or fantasy impossible.

But that first summer, Lee and his method went unchallenged. When his judgment was questioned, his lips would tighten and the color would go from his face. Everyone could see that an explosion was coming. Often it did come. Actors succumbed

* Harold Clurman (1901–1980) was a co-founder of The Group Theatre, as well as a director, critic and author, notably of the memoir, *The Fervent Years, The Group Theatre and the Thirties*, originally published in 1975 (editor's footnote).

to his emotionalism, even admired it. Facing his wrath, few would stand up for what they'd done. Gradually they became masochists; many seemed particularly to enjoy a good scolding from him. Lee was God almighty, he was always right, only he could tell if an actor had had it—the real thing—or not. To win Lee's favor and the reassurance it would convey was everyone's goal. No one doubted Lee those first months; I certainly didn't.

THE CELLULOID BRASSIÈRE

Andy Logan

F OR A JOURNALIST unwilling to interview Tennessee
Williams, who wrote the latest hit show, *The Glass Menagerie*,
the only alternative is giving up his press card. Fortunately,
Williams is an amiable and adaptable young man, unruffled
even by such experiences as being asked to pose for three news
photographers in a single morning. He told us, as he has told
other interviewers, that four years ago he was an usher at the
Strand Theatre. It turns out, however, that this was merely
an interlude between jobs as a Guild playwright (unsuccessful) and as a Hollywood script writer (unsuccessful). *Battle of
Angels* was the name of the Williams play the Guild put on,
and, though it starred Miriam Hopkins and was directed by
Margaret Webster, it folded up after the tryout in Boston. "I
never heard of an audience getting so infuriated," Williams
told us. "They hissed so loud you couldn't hear the lines, and
that made Miriam so mad that she began to scream her lines
above the hissing. Then they stamped their feet, and after
a while most of them got up and left, banging their seats
behind them. That play was, of course, a much better play
than this one. The thing is, you can't mix up sex and religion,
as I did in *Battle of Angels*, but you can always write safely
about mothers."

The mother Williams wrote about in *The Glass Menagerie* is his own. The play is mainly taken from life. "We moved to St. Louis when I was about thirteen," the author informed us. "We took an old house that just had windows at the front and back. My sister, who was a year older than I was, had a sad little shadowy room that looked out on an alley, so we painted it white for her, and she collected a lot of little glass animals and put them on the white shelves to brighten things up. It's something you remember. Especially if you're a playwright." A playwright Williams certainly is, the current show being the eighth he has written, not counting his work in Hollywood. He went out there straight from his run as a Strand usher, M-G-M having topped his old salary considerably (life is that way in the arts). They put him right to work on a Lana Turner picture the name of which he cannot remember—"I always thought of it as 'The Celluloid Brassière,'" he said—and then, when this project failed to work out, tried to assign him to a Margaret O'Brien script. When he had finished telling M-G-M what he thought of child actors, they barred him from the studio. He sat out the rest of his contract on the beach at Santa Monica, drawing two hundred and fifty dollars a week. That was when he started work on *The Glass Menagerie*. He finished it in Provincetown last summer. When he showed the manuscript to his agent, she said, "Well, let's get it typed, anyway."

Williams is a small, quiet man with rather close-clipped hair and a heart which is a little too unstable to allow him to be in the Army. Collectors of psychosomatic lore will be fascinated to learn that he was once paralyzed for two weeks, apparently as a gesture of protest against working in a shoe store; at any rate, when his parents told him he didn't have to go back to the shoe store, the paralysis went away. He seems to be pretty well relaxed now. "I never had a very hard time of it," he said, "so now that I'm about to have an easy time of it, it doesn't seem to make so much difference. In the last ten years I've nearly always done what I wanted, and when I needed money there were always things I could do—clerking or ushering. Sometimes it was a nuisance, taking time off from writing to make enough money to eat, but there are plenty of things about being successful that are a nuisance, too—those three photographers this morning, for instance."

THE NEW YORKER, APRIL 14, 1945

Marilyn Monroe and Susan Strasberg at The Actors Studio, 1955—Roy Schatt

RAINY DAY

Lillian Ross

S USAN STRASBERG, the seventeen-year-old who has made such a hit in *The Diary of Anne Frank*, stands just over five feet tall, weighs ninety-six pounds, has hazel eyes and ivory skin, and wears her light-brown hair shoulder length. We paid a call on her one rainy afternoon last week at the Strasberg apartment, in the West Eighties. Besides Susan, the family consists of her father, Lee Strasberg, who is a director and teacher of acting; her mother, Paula Miller, who is an actress; and her fourteen-year-old brother, Johnny, who is a student at the Bronx High School of Science. On the occasion of our visit, Susan was decked out in a royal-blue Chinese dress and blue harlequin glasses. She had a cold and was chewing a raspberry drop. The room in which we talked contained a fireplace, a piano, and an assortment of thoroughly sat-in armchairs, and was lined with books from floor to ceiling. "We're house-hunting for a brownstone," Susan said. "I love a house with steps inside; someone once told me it's a sign of youth. The piano is for Johnny and for parties. I started taking lessons years ago, but then Johnny took up singing. He has such a beautiful voice that I gave up music altogether. I suppose the competition was too much for me or something. Still, I hope to do a musical someday. Johnny is going to be a doctor. He claims he wants to be as far away from the theatre as possible. Oh, you've been highly complimented!"

The nature of the compliment eluded us until, turning round, we discovered that a large orange cat had stalked into the room, waving his tail aloft. "Meet Sweetie Pie Strasberg," Susan said. "He hardly ever comes out for strangers. For a long time, Sweetie Pie had the most terrible neurosis. He couldn't even meow, he was in such bad shape. Now he is almost perfectly adjusted." Sweetie Pie rubbed his back against Susan's legs and meowed. "You see what a good family life can do for a cat?" Susan inquired, and taking off her glasses, went on, "I'm nearsighted, but actually I'm not supposed to wear glasses for close-up things. Since I started working, I find myself wearing glasses more than I used to. I don't mind wearing glasses. Grace Kelly wears them, and that helps. If I weren't working today, I guess I'd be making icebox cookies or something. I love rain, especially when it's invigorating and clear. I was born right here in Manhattan, in 1938. I vary my age from sixteen to eighteen, depending on my mood and whom I'm with. My father says I must stop this business of having different ages. We've an actress friend who tells everyone, 'I'm thirty and proud of it,' but we all *know* she's thirty-five. From now on, I may just explain that I'm nine years younger than Audrey Hepburn, and let her carry the ball."

Susan has attended a total of nine schools, here and in California. She has studied ballet and commercial art but has had no formal training as an actress. "My parents don't believe in it for anyone under eighteen," she said. "Two years ago, I was offered a role in a play the Theatre de Lys was putting on, and since it was only for seven performances, my parents said O.K. The play was one of those symbolism things. I played the part of an up-and-coming French prostitute." Susan popped another drop into her mouth and continued, "Right after that, I got a chance to play Juliet in a television production of *Romeo and Juliet*. Then I went out to Hollywood and had a small part in *The Cobweb* and the part of the kid sister in *Picnic*. I like making movies, but I *love* the stage. Every night, I can hardly wait to go on. I guess I was bound to become an actress. When I was thirteen, we all went to Europe. We visited the castle of the real Juliet. When we got to the castle, I stepped out onto Juliet's balcony, and Mother has since told me that she had a premonition that someday I'd be playing Juliet. I asked her if she'd have a premonition that there would be a Kraft cheese commercial between the acts."

We were curious to know what Susan's response to opening night has been. "It was *hec*tic," she said. "I got to the theater early, and it seemed to me that everybody was running around screaming about telegrams and flowers. Johnny sent me some yellow dahlias and yellow roses in a Dutch shoe. And my parents sent me pink roses in a twin shoe with a quotation from Browning—that line about a man's reach having to exceed his grasp. And after the show they gave a party for me at Sardi's. It turned out I was *starved*. I ate fruit salad, ice cream, a ham-and-turkey sandwich on rye, some pizza, and some steak tartare, and I drank champagne. I slept like a log that night. Next day, I got up at one-thirty and had some orange juice and a vitamin pill and a wheat-germ pill and read the papers. First I read all the reviews of our play and then I read all the reviews of a movie

35

that had opened, and then Johnny came home from school and I sympathized with him about it."

A stocky man wearing horn-rimmed eyeglasses and tweeds came into the room and was introduced as Susan's father. "It's pouring outside, Father," Susan said. "Will it keep people away from the theatre?"

"It's only during heavy snows that people stay away," Mr. Strasberg said.

"I think it's a shame the way some people buy their tickets and then don't come," said Susan.

"They'll come," said her father.

THE NEW YORKER, OCTOBER 29, 1955

Paul Newman at The Actors Studio, 1955—Eve Arnold

James Dean, New York City, 1955—Dennis Stock

Sidney Poitier, early 1960s—Roy Schatt

BACKSTAGE AT
PLAYHOUSE 90

TIME

I T WAS TWO DAYS before showtime, and CBS's Hollywood Studio 31 was a reptile house of cables, clotted with men and monitors, cameras and booms, eight sets. "Tuesdays are miserable," a man explained. "The actors are just getting aware of the cameras and the feel of the set." This time, matters had got miserable well before Tuesday.

The play was *The Troublemakers*, a drama about college students who beat to death another boy because of some campus newspaper articles he had written.* Director John Frankenheimer (Williams, '51), a gangly TV veteran of 27, was disappointed from the start with George Bellak's TV adaptation of his original play. So Frankenheimer called in TV Author Rod (*Requiem for a Heavyweight*) Serling to doctor the script. With accomplished Actor Ben Gazzara to play the role, Frankenheimer wanted to expand the part of Stanley, the dead boy's roommate, who makes an effort to stop the fatal roughhouse, then suffers with a conscience-driven urge to tell all. "I want to be conscious of Benny Gazzara every minute,"

---

*   Drawn from a real-life case at Dartmouth, where eight students ganged up on ex-G.I. Ray Cirrotta and left him badly beaten. Several hours later he died.

said Frankenheimer. "This is the most creative actor I've ever worked with."

Serling had hardly begun his suturing job when—only six days before showtime—Producer Martin Manulis called his director. "We've had it," he said. "The Catholic press is saying we are doing a Communist play." All that had happened was that a columnist for some 45 Roman Catholic newspapers and magazines had written a story complaining that CBS was about to stage a play whose off-Broadway version in 1954 pleaded "for soft handling of suspected Communists." The story sent Madison Avenue into a flap, and ad agencies for the show's five sponsors talked of backing out. Officials at CBS rushed down a wad of proposed script changes.

"SHOOT TIGHT."

"Suddenly," said Frankenheimer, "it became very important to me to get this show on." In long conferences of Manulis, Frankenheimer, cast and whole production staff, ten lines were excised for appeasement purposes. So, by Miserable Tuesday, the unexpected crisis was over, and all the principals—Frankenheimer, Serling and Gazzara, Associate Director Jim Clark and Technical Director Brooks ("Nimble Fingers") Graham—could concentrate on the ordinary weekly Playhouse 90 crisis, the need to get out a show.

Crouching before the mobile monitor unit and chain-smoking ("Three packs of Sponsor Marlboros a day"), Frankenheimer bellowed comments to his cast and production staff. "That's the shot! It's beautiful. I love it." "It's sloppy. It stinks." "Shoot tight on someone in the foreground." He turned to direct a scene where Gazzara has just discovered that his roommate is dead. "Okay. Start Benny out of the bathroom, fellows. C'mon, I don't have much time." (Explained Frankenheimer on the side: "If you don't drive them, you have last-minute panic.")

Frankenheimer objected to a railing at the top of some dorm stairs. "Take that off!" There was trouble with the audio, but it was fixed with a "fishpole"—a long rod used to get the mike into niches the boom could not reach. An actor was not punching the victim realistically. A cable man stumbled into camera view. One by one, the mistakes were rehearsed away.

"PAN DOWN."

"Now let's go into the woods, fellows," said Frankenheimer, and the camera followed the director into one corner of the studio, where real trees had been wired upright for the "burial" scene. "Instead of a pine tree I want a tree with no leaves," Frankenheimer snapped. "Pull out this briar bush. This is supposed to be New England." The camera came in on the boys with the body. "Dump it face down," called John. "Pan down on the body. Good. I like it."

After lunch, Frankenheimer moved into the control booth, where the action could be viewed only as it looks on the TV screen, put on his headphones, and yelled: "Take it from the top ... Settle down in the studio. I can't hear the dialogue." He watched a chilling scene in which four liquored-up Saunders College students prance wildly around the young man they are about to kill in a spasm of inchoate brutality. "All of you are too drunk in that scene," Frankenheimer said into a microphone that blared his commands all over the huge studio. "You haven't had that much to drink yet. Benny, take your walk again, please. Fellows, wait for your cue, then come in like gangbusters." Later, in a Gazzara love scene with Barbara Rush, china in a sideboard came crashing down. "John, that's a maniacal piece of furniture," Gazzara complained. The piece was promptly fixed.

On Wednesday, with only a day to go, Producer Manulis sat taking notes: too much blood in the bathroom; too many "Gods and God-awfuls" in the script; Harry Guardino should chuck his cigar for a cigarette, because "we sell cigarettes here"; "Hershey Bar" must become "candy bar"; Mary Astor ought to play her scenes without makeup; Gazzara was crying too loudly, in Act 4. The director found the ceiling in the police station "too beautiful. I want it cruddy," decreed Frankenheimer. "Put sprinklers on it."

"NOW CLOSE IN."

At dress rehearsal, only three hours before showtime, Frankenheimer fired frenzied notes to his script girl: "The star shots look terrible. The music wasn't on time. Ben's collar should be neat; he looks like a thug. Keenan looked hypnotized. We have chaos." But the chaos went smoothly. "Watch the shadows," Nimble Fingers Graham added. Frankenheimer said, "Arc to the right. Now close in. Ready Camera Two. Standby Four. Take Four," and snapped his fingers crisply—each snap the sign for a camera change. "The murder scene went fine, fellows," said Nimble Fingers. "But I saw a boom in the bath." Someone was running behind a window that was supposed to be four flights up. "We've got some mighty tall actors," Frankenheimer cracked. "Stay dead longer," he instructed Jack Mullaney, the murdered student, "then tiptoe out of the studio."

With only an hour to go, Frankenheimer addressed the cast and crew once more. The noise in the final scene, he said to the camera crewmen, "was a disgrace—it will kill the whole show." Frankenheimer dressed down Gazzara again about his shirt. "John, I'll look adorable," Ben promised. Barbara Rush was playing the café scene with too much "sympathy and not relating to Ben." Barbara replied: "I try to get anger by trying to think of—if my child were killed." Frankenheimer blanched. "That's what's wrong. You are being a mother. Anger is a lover's emotion." Then Frankenheimer gave everyone his blessings. "This has been a hellish week. What we have is really good. Don't be afraid to have fun with it." Handsome Barbara Rush promised: "Oh, John, I'll try so hard. I've got to merge anger and relating."

"CUE THE BOYS."

Fifteen minutes to go. T. D. Graham went back to his panel to match cameras and to check video, tapes, film, music, lights, master control and audio levels. Five minutes. "Positions, please," Frankenheimer called. Then "One minute, and good luck!" The red second hand on the big clock above the monitors moved to 6:30, Hollywood time. Frankenheimer ordered: "Up on One and cue the boys." Then, in an aside: "I'm oblivious from now on. I'm not aware that anyone else is watching it." The

45

first commercial ended, and there was a slow dissolve on the body of the boy as they dumped him in the woods. "Keep that sonuvabitch dead. Pan up. Fishpole, get the hell out of there! I see you. Who's that heavy-handed guy on the music? Don't hit Ben with the camera, Number Two. Dammit, you just did hit him! There's a big boom shadow on Barbara's face."

In the control booth, at the climactic scene, when Gazzara defied the bullies with a baseball bat, Frankenheimer went to his knees to call camera changes, his fingers snapping with a crapshooter's passion. The final scene approached. He whispered urgently to camera crews: "Noise! Take it easy, you have lots of time." The scene went smoothly. "Ready to dissolve to black, black!" The screen went black. Off came the headset. Frankenheimer leaped out of his seat and watched the assistant director signal the credits. "Gotta get 'em all in, Jim, you gotta!" Then he turned to Martin Manulis and quietly shook hands on Playhouse 90's best show of the season. Only minutes later, the sets had been struck, and everyone had gone home.

DECEMBER 2, 1957

Sidney Lumet directing Lorne Greene, 1953—Roy Schatt

THE OUTSKIRTS:
OTHER MEN'S WOMEN

Gina Telaroli

> Talk about your subway, talk about your "el"
> Talk about your streetcar lines as well
> But when you're living out where the fields are green
> You've got to go home on the 5.15

I T'S THE AUTUMN of 1930 and a #103 steam engine on the San Diego & Arizona Railway chugs to life. Just as it gets going, the shot cuts upwards, to the top of the moving train and a well-dressed man running under the hazy California sky towards the camera. He stops at the top of the frame, waves his arm up and exclaims: "Hiya gang!"

For a split second it is almost as if he's addressing the audience—and in a way he is, the train-top actor is none other than James Cagney in one of his earliest roles—until the camera cuts down to the train's operators and best pals Bill and Jack. Grant Withers's Bill joins Cagney's Eddie atop the moving locomotive—"Come on up here and get a bit of fresh air!"— and the two shoot the shit, talking dames and ducking under an approaching bridge. Bill offers Eddie a piece of gum and a catchphrase—"Have a little chew on me!"—and gets back inside the still-moving train. It's a mostly meaningless conversation, the scene functioning more for its form, for the movement and energy it generates. The director, William A. Wellman, isn't telling a story as much as he's creating an atmosphere, a sense of being, a way of life.

The opening scenes of *Other Men's Women* (1931), first released under the title *The Steel Highway*, were shot in Jacumba, California, a small unincorporated community near the Mexican border. It was Wellman's second time in the area; he had last been there in 1928 shooting the train scenes of his feature *Beggars of Life*, based on Jim Tully's hobo memoir about riding the rails. It was a time his lead actress Louise Brooks would later recount when she wrote "On Location with Billy Wellman" for *Focus on Film* in the winter of 1972:

> He [Bert Vaughn, a wealthy land developer from San Diego] had built Jacumba in 1919 as a summer resort where the farmers of the Imperial Valley might escape from the desert heat, and bathe in its mineral springs. Situated on the railroad running between San Diego and Yuma, it was an ideal location for Beggars of Life because only four trains ran daily on its track, leaving many hours free for our private freight train to go before the camera. Photographically, spinning down the mountains among the deep canyons, the track was superb.

Wellman's breakthrough, Oscar-winning picture *Wings* (1927), had been a very different affair, with extensive rehearsals, hundreds of extras including some 300 pilots, technical feats of fancy, and Hollywood's "It girl" Clara Bow as the female lead. The film shared a set with another Paramount production,

Victor Fleming's *The Rough Riders*, which featured then 21-year-old, Illinois-born Mary Astor. Later, in her 1971 autobiography *A Life on Film*, she would write:

> Between technical delays and bad weather, the two companies
> had time for a great deal of fraternizing. Romances broke out like
> heat rashes, there were a couple of weddings, at least one divorce,
> and I'm sure a few local irate husbands and outraged parents. If
> there were roughhousing and drunken brawls and somebody got
> hauled off to jail, they were sprung the next day. You just can't
> hold up production, you know!

It's because of *Wings*, and his own history as a pilot, that Wellman is most often remembered for his cinematic obsession with the sky but, as if to show why, his films equally obsess on the ground and the feet that stand there. From the leg up, the bodies he captured were bodies in motion, bodies at work. A waitress gets her ass slapped. A couple walks down the railroad tracks. A stuttering landlady throws her drunken tenant down the porch stairs.

A young housewife, Lily (a now 24-year-old Mary Astor), is icing a cake when her husband, Regis Toomey's Jack, brings a drunken and now homeless Bill home with him to dry out and get his act together. The calm and composed Jack fades into the background as Lily and Bill play in the hot California sun, digging holes, planting sweet peas, singing tunes, fighting in the yard, giving each other haircuts, fixing buttons, and unexpectedly falling in love. In a Wellman movie, it's labor that bonds characters together.

An on-screen love triangle was not an unfamiliar scenario for Colorado-born Withers who had spent part of his twenty-second year on the set of John Ford's 1927 film *Upstream*. Formerly a newspaperman and oil salesman, it was Withers's first feature role, a role that saw him playing a knife-thrower in a two-man, one-woman vaudeville act. Withers's character is the third, longing for his female co-star who is ever so unfortunately with his male co-star. Ford foregrounds his film in the romantic entanglements before effortlessly easing out of them. But where Ford lets the plot dwindle, Wellman never pretends to care. The necessary narrative may forge ahead like a locomotive, moving at a breakneck pace...

> *Bill and Lily kiss. Bill flees. Jack and Bill fight. Jack is injured. Bill is drunk. Bill learns that Jack is blind because of their fight. Jack decides his life is worthless. A storm threatens to destroy a bridge. Bill decides to risk death in order to save the bridge. Jack decides to risk death in order to save the bridge. Jack hits Bill and pushes him out of the train before the train is swept into the river as the bridge collapses. Time passes. Bill and Lily reunite at the diner from the opening scene.*

... but it's only when the train leaves the station, when the plot pulls away, that the bread and butter of *Other Men's Women* is revealed; the moments of leisure, labor, and other bits of business; the outskirts. It's typical Wellman to surround one line of necessary dialogue, or an important conversation, with a bustling scene, the information threatening to get lost in the hubbub.

Towards the end of the film Jack sits with his former co-workers drinking coffee and laughing. Torrential rain is pouring down outside. The men sing a rousing round of Stanley Murphy and Henry I. Marshall's "On the 5.15." They catch up, drink more coffee, and somewhere amid all of that there's an exchange about Bill wanting to save a rain-threatened bridge, which the now blind Jack overhears. Jack sets off, fumbling his way through the drenched rail yard, Wellman spending more time on his journey, on watching his body feel its way through the space, at one point almost crashing into the camera, than on any kind of what or why.

Bodily loss was something Pittsburgh-born, University of Pittsburgh grad Regis Toomey was accustomed to. It was the loss of his singing voice in the late twenties that took him from the stages of Broadway and Europe to Hollywood and into his first screen role in Roland's West's early sound film, 1929's *Alibi*, the experiment of which critic Elliot Stein summed up perfectly in *Cinema: A Critical Dictionary*:

> The distorted sets, odd angles and restless camera make it West's most Germanic work.

In *Other Men's Women*, Wellman would expand upon and shift the frenetic energy of films like *Alibi*, squeezing out any harsh European hoo-ha, twisting it all up in the dusty suburbs of America's West, making sure he could shoot the way he wanted, as he told Richard Schickel for his book *The Men Who Made the Movies*:

> When we first started [sound], the booms were camouflaged. They hung from the chandeliers or something, you had to get

your action underneath there. That burned me up—you can't make a picture that way. You've got to have some flow. So I came in and I said, "I got news for you sound men this morning. I'm moving that god-damned mike." And I got my grip, got me a big high ladder and went and took [the mike] and put it on the end of a broomstick. And I moved it and it worked.

The result, in this film and others from the pre-Code period, is a dizzying energy, his actors moving, inhabiting, exploring. Scene after scene the air reeks of a spirit of discovery. A spirit which Astor, somewhat cynically, recalled later in her life:

I was in a piece of cheese called *Other Men's Women*. In it there were some damn good actors—James Cagney, Joan Blondell—in small parts.

But small parts are a Wellman specialty. And like another lovelorn blonde, Dorothy Malone's Marylee in Douglas Sirk's *Written on the Wind* (1956), Blondell's Marie is painted—slutty, drunk, hot-tempered, creating unnecessary drama that leads the protagonists away from happiness—as a kind of villain. But even as the other characters speak badly of Marie, Wellman loves her dearly.

And Marie loves Bill. She loves him goofy and drunk. She loves him dancing. She loves him tossing out bullshit that she lovingly refuses to bite: "If you offer me a chew of gum now, I'll knock your block off!"

Immediately after Jack's injury Wellman cuts to Bill and Marie completely sloshed at the dancehall. The plotted point is that Bill's doing badly but the camera suggests otherwise, as it quickly moves in for a long close-up of the two, watching them in awe, in admiration, Bill in profile while Marie looks out with smeared lipstick, tangled hair, and a dazed expression. They cry and laugh together, experiencing life in all of its abundance. The constantly evolving expression on Blondell's face, from pure joy to pure despair, perfectly mirrors Wellman's philosophy of moviemaking, of what brought him back to the railways of Jacumba, to movie set after movie set, which he expressed in his aptly titled autobiography *A Short Time for Insanity*:

> Day in and day out, year after year, you are crying or you are laughing, you are tense or you are relaxed, your emotions are turned on and off like a spigot, and you must be careful not to become so calloused that when the real thing happens it hasn't been robbed of its vitality. A motion picture company lives hard and plays hard, and they better or they will go nuts.

.　　.　　.　　.　　.

In 1944, 36-year-old Mary Astor would find herself going a little nuts playing the mother of 27-year-old Lucille Bremer and 22-year-old Judy Garland in *Meet Me in St. Louis*, commencing what she would call her "Mothers for Metro" period. It was a striking change for the admitted alcoholic who had a few years earlier been embroiled in a cheating scandal and headline-making custody battle for her daughter.

Regis Toomey drifted through life as a character actor working with everyone (Hawks, Hitchcock, Borzage) and anyone

(Ulmer, Fregonese, Jerry Lewis) for the next fifty-six years. Toomey's last film role would be in 1987's *Evil Town*, a film about an old doctor conducting horrific experiments on young people passing through the area. He passed away four years later at the age of ninety-three.

Post-*Other Men's Women*, Grant Withers would hang out in leading-man roles for a minute or two before he found himself banished to supporting roles and bit parts in westerns and other B-movies and serials. He had a contract at Republic Studios for ten years and often found work with old friends John Wayne and John Ford.

In 1959, at the age of fifty-four and after years of ill-health, he overdosed on barbiturates. Withers's suicide note read: "Please forgive me, my family. I was so unhappy. It's better this way."

The 2010 United States Census reported that Jacumba had a population of 561. The hot springs still exist, as does a hotel, but a quick look online suggests that these days, people mostly go there to take photos of the uninhabited, rocky landscape, including the abandoned railcars that are strewn along the now-defunct tracks.

THE PETRIFIED FOREST

Jorge Luis Borges

I T IS COMMONLY OBSERVED that allegories are tolerable in direct proportion to their inconsistency and vagueness, which does not signify an apology for inconsistency and vagueness but, rather, a proof—a sign, at least—that the genre of allegory is a mistake. "The genre of allegory," I said, not the components or suggestions of allegory. (The best and most famous allegory, *The Pilgrim's Progress from This World to That Which Is to Come*, by Puritan visionary John Bunyan, must be read as a novel, not as a prophecy; but if we eliminate all the symbolic justifications, the book will be absurd.)

The measure of allegory in *The Petrified Forest* is perhaps exemplary: light enough so as not to invalidate the drama's reality, substantial enough so as not to invalidate the drama's improbabilities. On the other hand, two or three weaknesses or pedantries in the dialogue continue to annoy me: a confused theological theory of neuroses, the summary (totally and minutely inaccurate) of a poem by T.S. Eliot, the forced allusions to Villon, Mark Twain and Billy the Kid, contrived to make the audience feel erudite in recognizing those names.

Once the allegorical motive is dismissed or relegated to a secondary level, the plot of *The Petrified Forest*—the magical influence of approaching death on a random group of men and women—seems admirable to me. In this film, death works like hypnosis or alcohol: it brings the recesses of the soul into the light of day. The characters are extraordinarily distinct: the smiling, anecdotal grandfather, who sees everything as performance and greets the dissolution and bullets as a happy return to his youth; the weary gunman Mantee, as resigned to killing (and making others kill) as the rest of us are to dying; the imposing and absolutely vain banker with a diplomat's air of a great man of our conservative party; the young Gabrielle, who is given to attributing her romantic turn of mind to her French blood and her qualities as good *ménagère* to her Yankee origins; the poet, who advises her to reverse the terms of that attribution, which is so American—and so mythical.

I do not recall any other movies by Archie Mayo. This film (along with *The Passing of the Third Floor Back*) is one of the most intense I have seen.

Sur, September 1936
Translated by Ronald Christ

ACE IN THE HOLE:
NOIR IN BROAD DAYLIGHT

Molly Haskell

B ILLY WILDER'S *Ace in the Hole* almost requires an honorary expansion of the term film noir. There are no private eyes in seedy offices or femmes fatales lurking in the shadows of neon-lit doorways, no forces of evil arrayed against a relatively honorable hero. This emotional snake pit, the darkest of Wilder's dark meditations on American folkways, takes place under the relentless sun of the flat New Mexican desert. The noir is interior—inside a mountain tunnel where a man is trapped and suffocating, and inside the mind of a reporter rotting from accumulated layers of self-induced moral grime.

The 1951 movie, fascinating in the sweep and savagery of its indictment, and a flop when it opened (and again when it was released as *The Big Carnival*), points to the direction noir would take in the fifties, hiding in broad daylight in the films of Alfred Hitchcock, Nicholas Ray, Douglas Sirk. But if Hitchcock diabolically upended our expectations of the leading man, Wilder went much, much further. This satire of the media circus that would envelop us all goes beyond noir into saeva indignatio, and beyond Swift into something more intensely and disturbingly personal. Rarely, if ever, have there been such brutally antipathetic leads in a mainstream film as Kirk Douglas's scoop-or-die reporter and Jan Sterling's breathtakingly callous victim's wife. However prophetic Wilder's vision of a press and a public drunk on sensation, this issue ends up seeming almost peripheral to two main characters so monstrous in their mutual, and mutually despising, selfishness that it's astonishing the movie got released at all.

BENT REPORTER, DESPERATE FOR A SCOOP

Fresh from his star-making turn as the self-promoting prizefighter in *Champion* (1949), a ferociously determined Douglas gives one of his great over-the-top, sadomasochistic performances as Chuck Tatum, bent reporter (that he's a liar, a fabricator, and an adulterer just begins to count the ways), desperate for a scoop, a ticket back to a big-city newspaper, who winds up in the hick town of Albuquerque. Before landing him in the newspaper office, an extended opening scene features one of cinema's great entrances: Douglas's convertible, having broken down in the desert, is being towed in to the local shop as he sits like a catbird in the driver's seat, reading a newspaper, with the camera tracking alongside. The image is that of a man both crippled and defiant: to be carless—see *Sunset Boulevard* (1950)—is to be emasculated, but this born opportunist and exploiter has turned the truck driver into his charioteer. Having now acquainted himself with the local paper, Tatum strides into its storefront office and, with characteristic chutzpah, condescends to the locals—"How," he says to a Native American, and sneers at the secretary's handmade sampler ("Tell the Truth")—before penetrating the office of the kindly editor-publisher, played by Porter Hall. In an outrageous Wilderian aria of simultaneous self-promotion and self-contempt, he makes his pitch: "I can handle big news," he boasts; all he needs is "just one good beat," as he comes down in price—"Fifty dollars ... Forty-five dollars." There is something already frightening, if funny, in the mixture of self-abasement and aggression. It's the self-abasement that is the aggression, as if he's getting the jump on you by saying the very worst, bragging about what a liar he is, even as he confesses each sordid detail of his firings from various newspapers. He talks himself into and out of a job several times over and is finally hired for sixty bucks.

As he settles in, we can't help but respond in some degree to his abject down-and-outness, his hunger and desperation, not to mention the New York hustler vibe he brings to this white-bread environment, where there are no pickles, no chopped liver (a sly reference to Douglas's—and Wilder's—Jewishness?), no Yogi Berra, where never is heard a discouraging word and the "Tell the Truth" sampler reeks of small-town naïveté.

GIVES FLOOZIES A BAD NAME

Then the "big story" arrives, or rather the little story that Tatum, practicing journalism as extreme sport, manipulates into a national scoop. Leo Minosa (Richard Benedict), the man trapped in the mountain tunnel, was digging for relics to sell at the trading post/café he runs with his wife, Lorraine, the sort of bottle blonde who gives floozies a bad name. The script, written by Wilder, Walter Newman, and Lesser Samuels and nominated for an Academy Award, was the first that Wilder directed after his official breakup with his longtime coscenarist, Charles Brackett (somehow one can't imagine the writer who withdrew from *Double Indemnity* (1944) because it was too lurid and unpleasant engaging enthusiastically in this project). The story, inspired by a 1925 incident in which a Kentucky man, trapped in a mine, was turned by reporters into a nationwide sensation, was given to Wilder in the form of a treatment by radio writer Newman. Samuels, a playwright who'd shared an Oscar nomination with Joe Mankiewicz the previous year for the script of *No Way Out*, was brought in for a polish. But Wilder, now his own producer, upped the ante exponentially. And to make the story even juicier—or more ominous—the mountain becomes a sacred Native American site whose offended spirits may be visiting retribution on poor Leo, or, as Tatum's headline has it, "The Curse of the Seven Vultures." To add to the sense of desecration of a native shrine, an indigenous woman, virtually faceless and voiceless, periodically appears, hunched in prayer.

Leo's wife, the coarse and chillingly indifferent Lorraine, wants only to flee this dump and the husband who "rescued" her from her dubious past, but she is persuaded to stay—more accurately, battered into submission—by the even greedier and more single-minded Tatum. In a scene that makes Jimmy Cagney's grapefruit assault on Mae Clarke look like friendly teasing, Douglas slaps her, hard, on both cheeks. Her later response? "Don't ever slap me again." He convinces her not only to stay on as the concerned wife but to go to church and pray, overriding her objection. "I don't go to church," she says, in one of the movie's greatest one-liners. "Kneeling bags my nylons."

As a result of the front-page stories Tatum is putting out and the wire services are picking up, the excavation project turns into a carnivalesque free-for-all, as tourists, then politicians, then reporters, then sundry performers all gravitate to the site for their own varied and unsavory purposes. A fee is charged, a Ferris wheel set up, with Wilder gleefully orchestrating what would only later be called a "media frenzy." Tatum has bribed the local sheriff (an excellently slimy Ray Teal) into making sure he, Tatum, has exclusive rights to the story. The reporters who arrive are no better, it's intimated, than Tatum; he just got there first. So far so bad, in an ordinary, predictable, corrupt, commonplace display of greed and sensation-mongering. But then Tatum does the unforgivable. He is presented by the contractor with two alternative rescue plans, and he opts for the one that will take six days rather than a few hours, letting the sheriff lean on the reluctant contractor, who owes his position to him.

GRUBBY, POSTWAR AMERICA

Wilder's vision of corruption seems to take in the whole spectrum of grubby, postwar America, with its loss of moral imperatives, its return to normalcy after the excitement of the war years. He plants his finger firmly and prophetically on the pulse of the new excitement, an addiction to the breaking story that television would create and feed to a nation of adrenaline junkies. Already in the squawking, hawking opportunists are our own telegenic communicators in embryonic form, the self-promoting reporters donning bedouin robes or Muslim chadors or hurricane slickers to provide twenty-four-hour coverage of themselves at the ego-center of hot spots and sleazy "human interest" tabloid stories. Stories whose staying power is manufactured, stories stretched out beyond any "human interest" at all, simply because they are scary, scandalous, sordid, or just bad, and fill the airspace until the next bad story arrives—or until the anniversary of an old one. Bad news, as Tatum points out, sells, and the no news that is good news to most people is bad news for the reporter. Forty-five people trapped in a mine isn't as good as one individual, who can be probed and dramatized and identified with; on the other hand, death is a bummer. So the reporter is genuinely horrified when it looks like Leo may actually die.

In a harrowing scene in the mine's interior, Leo asks for a priest, wails for his Lorraine, while still trusting Tatum, who, eyes blazing in the darkness with zeal and fear, promises he'll be out in twelve hours. He asks the contractor to switch to the faster rescue option, but it is too late. It's at this point that Tatum degenerates from a rattlesnake into a murderer, and the movie takes on a Grand Guignol aspect, with Tatum's self-loathing turning both homicidal and suicidal.

The cynical hero who's ready to sell his soul is, of course, trademark Wilder. Protagonists who "do what they have to do" in difficult circumstances, most notably William Holden's screenwriter/kept man in *Sunset Boulevard* and his black-marketeer war prisoner in *Stalag 17* (1953), draw on Wilder's own experience as a dance-hall gigolo in twenties Berlin. But these antiheroes are a mixture of corruption and decency, never quite as cynical as they seem; light generally shines through in the form of empathy, even a final act of remorse and redemption. Douglas would go on to have a long and colorful career but was often, as his role in *Ace in the Hole* may indicate, more interesting as a heavy than as a hero. Rarely has a star played as thoroughly nasty a specimen with such relish. What makes Douglas's Chuck Tatum so unusual is this absence of any redeeming gesture. His ultimate fetching of the priest doesn't feel noble, only desperate. Yes, there's a small self-sacrificial moment at the end, when he puts the young photographer on the right track, confesses, and insists that the newspaper tell the whole story. But the awareness is nothing new: he's always known what he was. It's part of the self-loathing that seems almost to have propelled Tatum from the beginning, and of which his death-wish plea to report the truth is a kind of final spasm.

Also, even in Wilder movies, there are usually other characters who elicit our sympathy. With the exception of Leo's parents, the honorable editor, and Tatum's reporter-sidekick (Bob Arthur)—all minor characters—there's no one in the gathering of vultures who comes off with a shred of humanity.

For once, it's hard to quarrel with Bosley Crowther's original assessment, that Wilder's "yarn ... presents not only a distortion of journalistic practice but something of a dramatic grotesque." It's just that we've caught up with and adapted to the grotesque, may even find something perversely satisfying in a film so resolutely uncommercial. Yes, Wilder risks drowning in his own cynicism, choking on his own bile, but we are now the rubberneckers at a spectacle only too ready to go down in flames of self-destruction. However rancid the taste left by the movie's exceptionally ghoulish portrait of America, there is a kind of awesome, irresistibly noxious power in the relationship between Tatum and Lorraine. Have any movie couple ever hated each other so much? The mounting intensity gives rise to a loathing so fierce it takes on erotic overtones. Jan Sterling's jaded Lorraine is about as uncompromisingly bad and unlikable as a woman in a major role can be, and Sterling plays her with tremendous nervy gusto. She's funny, as monomaniacal as Tatum, and relentlessly tawdry. A smart cookie playing dumb, she's even colder and more self-centered than Tatum, remembering years by the color of her hair ("In '45, I was a redhead"), and shameless to the bitter end in her scorn and indifference toward her suffering husband.

Wilder's women, no less than his men, are alter egos, often taking the fall for the guilt or anxiety that men are loath to acknowledge. The strain of misogyny that runs through many of Wilder's films can be a conduit and a cover for self-contempt. A director's anxiety about his own waning powers feeds and colors the coruscating portrait of the aging diva played by Gloria Swanson in *Sunset Boulevard*. The sleazy image of the dance-hall prostitute infuses Sterling's coarse Lorraine. The prize for infamy goes to Chuck Tatum, but both characters bear the brunt of Wilder's angst—not just corruption, anxiety, but the survivor's guilt of a man whose family died in Auschwitz. Here, as an innocent man is snuffed in a cave that bears a metaphoric resemblance to a concentration camp, the survivors look at each other with the venom of self-hatred, mirroring too closely each other's venality.

WHAT MAKES
A SAD HEART SING:
SOME CAME RUNNING

Michael Koresky

"THE MORE BEAUTIFUL everything is the more it will hurt without you." That's Jerry Mulligan (Gene Kelly) to Lise Bouvier (Leslie Caron) in *An American in Paris* (1951), and a more succinct expression of the exquisite fatalism that runs through Vincente Minnelli's cinema could hardly be found. Even if happy endings are on the horizon, as they tend to be in the director's musicals, they are desperately hard-won, last-minute resolutions that cannot erase the darkness and longing of what came before: consider the patriarch's abrupt decision not to relocate the family to New York in *Meet Me in St. Louis* (1944) or the eleventh-hour romantic reversals in *An American in Paris* and *Gigi* (1958). The turnarounds are so quick they almost feel like waking from dreams—and maybe they are.

Minnelli's melodramas, which comprised about a third of his output (comedies being the final third), are a different story. The genre allowed Minnelli to burrow into dark crevices untouched by the light cast by any possible deus ex machina. Without forgoing his extraordinary eye for meticulous visual composition, Minnelli created dramas of futility, longing, and disappointment that shot to the heart of a mid-century America that, despite postwar triumph and rapid economic growth, was impaired by parochial and insular forces of its own making.

No Minnelli melodrama is more elegantly conceived—or less emotionally forgiving—than 1958's *Some Came Running*, his headlong dive into the chaos of wrecked, impossible lives. As in 1956's *Tea and Sympathy*, his characters are doomed to unhappiness for reasons both socially conditioned and psychologically constructed. A film of pessimism without misanthropy, *Some Came Running* operates in a similar register to so many screen melodramas of the 1950s that seemed eager to diagnose small-town USA hypocrisies and small-mindedness and the discomfort of living as an outsider amid the oppressive atmospheres they create, from *All That Heaven Allows* (1955) and *Picnic* (1955) to *Peyton Place* (1957) and *No Down Payment* (1957). Minnelli's film is the least forthrightly soap operatic of these. Set in 1948, a time rocked by postwar economic and moral uncertainty, it's a dark-toned, Technicolor vision of an America split, Edward Hopper-like, between the false sunshine of daytime and the vivid threat of night.

Pruned way down from novelist James Jones's mammoth— and poorly reviewed—1,266-page follow-up to his 1951 novel *From Here to Eternity*, *Some Came Running* (1953) uses every frame of its 135 minutes to communicate the despondency of lives that don't fit together. Witnessing the interactions of any of the film's various incongruous pairs of characters is like watching a square peg and round hole endlessly circle one another. There's Dave Hirsh (Frank Sinatra), who, as the film opens, has just returned to his dreaded hometown of Parkman, Indiana, on an

68

overnight bus from Chicago. Wearing his army uniform, with its beige, flat-front dreariness, he looks skinny, formless; when he asks the bus driver if he wants to get a beer, the response is a shrug and a wake-up call, "Nothing open yet anyway." Then there's Ginny (Shirley MacLaine), the blowsy good-time gal from a few seats back on the bus. Waking up with smeared lipstick and rouge, she has to remind Dave that he invited her along. He gives her the brush-off ("Sorry, but a guy gets loaded and meets a girl, and you know…"), shooing her away with fifty, guilty bucks, but she stays in town anyway.

Soon enough, Dave will also meet hearty, tipsy professional gambler Bama Dillert (Dean Martin, at his toothsome best), who approaches him at local bar Smitty's with an invitation to his regular poker night. A little bit of a devil, a little bit of a dandy, Bama's most memorable trait is that he refuses to doff his Stetson, even in the presence of ladies. (Godard famously referenced Bama in 1963's *Contempt* when Michel Piccoli refused to take off his hat even in the bathtub, hoping to evoke cool cat Martin.) This model of callow masculinity rounds out *Some Came Running*'s odd, unofficial trio in style, each of them one drink or trick away from the gutter. The friendship between Dave and Bama results in one of the film's chewiest twosomes: at times they seem as unhealthy a team as Dorian Gray and Lord Henry, while at others they're nurturing bosom buddies.

In a film punctiliously designed in contrasts, the rowdy, socially untethered Ginny and Bama are the nocturnal antipodes to the characters who embody "respectable" society and thus represent Dave's past and possible future. It isn't long before Dave gets a visit in his hotel room from his estranged older brother, Frank (Arthur Kennedy), an upstanding jeweler who serves on the board of a local bank. Offered whiskey, Frank protests that it's 10:30 in the morning. "I don't watch the clock," snorts Dave, still resentful toward his brother for having put him into a charity boarding school when they were young. Though unimpressed as ever at Frank's upward mobility, achieved by marrying the wealthy Agnes (Leora Dana), Dave agrees to visit Frank and Agnes in their palatial, plantation-like home. In these luxurious walls, he meets Agnes's acquaintance Gwen French (Martha Hyer), a high school teacher and the daughter of an esteemed local professor. Having arrived in town with a sack of clothes that's mostly filled with books by Faulkner, Steinbeck, and Wolfe, Dave is a former writer haunted by his early novel's lack of success and an unfinished manuscript, so he's both pleased and repelled by the fact that Gwen is a fan of his writing. She flatters him with her sharp-edged compliments: his first book "might have lacked something in craftsmanship, but was a powerful study in rejection," she handily claims. The two get closer, but she's an intellectual who wants Dave to like her for her mind, rejecting his erotic advances and staving him off so much that he falls madly in love with her.

Minnelli's film is ruthless in its insistence on each of its characters' unhappiness, even after it dangles hope in front of them. Each of Minnelli's CinemaScope frames communicates the distance between people—these aren't pretty frames, they're admittances of desperation. Prim and cerebral, Gwen is the antithesis in every way of Ginny, who begins to pursue Dave with the same agonized hopefulness with which he pursues the unattainable professor's daughter. Minnelli highlights the women's dramatic contrasts most vividly after Gwen drops Dave near Smitty's following their first date. Inside the bar, he runs into Ginny, wearing a pink dress, chunky necklace, enough rouge to fill a Rothko, and a red carnation in her hair that all but dwarfs her head.

Despite such extravagant visual cues, Ginny comes off neither tawdry nor cheap. She's a miraculous creation of both Minnelli and MacLaine, an entirely appealing figure whose buoyancy and gentleness help the character overcome her essentially pathetic nature and push away any outworn "hooker with a heart of gold" clichés. Ginny often disappears from the narrative in the first half of the film, which is an effective approach, as it forces the viewer to fill in the blanks about what she must be doing in the dark alleys of Parkman by night, while also making us genuinely miss her presence—in ways that the other characters, prone to pushing her around, never seem to. Late in the film, when Ginny confronts Gwen in her classroom, hoping to lay claim to Dave for her own, she looks completely awkward—a clumsy stork desperately trying to tiptoe through a tulip garden—yet she's touching in her drive to do the right thing.

At first, Dave simply ignores Ginny's entreaties, but Bama is actively dehumanizing towards her, continually referring to the sweet-hearted woman as a "pig"; to people of upstanding stock like Frank and Gwen she's simply invisible. MacLaine absorbs every slight and insult, yet used to a rough-and-tumble existence, she proves resilient. She often appears either sweetly oblivious to—or perhaps unperturbed by—how others perceive her. Yet at the same time she's nobody's fool. In a bravura night-club sequence, MacLaine, moving in rhythmic counterpoint to Minnelli's fluidly tracking camera, gets up and starts an impromptu sing-along to a performance of "After You've Gone," nearly drowning out the male trio at the mic with her screeching caterwaul. Her red dress stands out crassly, courageously from the club's buttoned-down, shadowy atmosphere, a rosy smudge against a charcoal canvas.

Dave ultimately warms to Ginny, though whether it's out of habit, pity, or just an impulsive rebound after a final rejection from Gwen, is left poignantly unclear. Of course, it's too late for a happy ending. *Some Came Running* climaxes with one of Minnelli's most enthralling set pieces, set against Parkman's Centennial carnival celebration, an occasion as bedecked with garish color as it is mercilessly grim. Always devoted to the potential for mise-en-scène to hold darkness and light at once, exhilaration and terror, Minnelli was particularly exacting in this sequence. In an apocryphal tale, according to an actor on-set, Indiana native Denny Miller, the director demanded that the crew take down the entire Ferris wheel—and move it a foot. Scrupulously designed even as it seems like everything's about to fly off its hinges, the carnival is the dazzling horror of America itself, a revel in freneticism that spirals out into violence. Raymond, Ginny's jealous gangster boyfriend from Chicago, has returned, stalking the grounds. The past—both the historical past, represented by the false American cheer of the patriotic celebration, and the personal past, embodied by the looming, gun-toting Raymond—has returned, teeth bared and out for blood.

In someone else's melodrama, tragedy might lead to inspiration. A writer whose words have had little impact on the world or even noticeable effect on other people, Dave might have used his experiences to come to some greater understanding about his outcast status or perhaps about the class distinctions that had led to violence and sadness. Yet *Some Came Running*, like other Minnelli films that penetrate the interior worlds of frustrated artists (Jerry Mulligan, Vincent van Gogh, *Tea and Sympathy*'s Tom Lee), isn't preoccupied with art as redemption. Rather, it's informed by the psychological trauma that comes with aspiring to creative greatness. Art can try and make the world beautiful, but that will only make it hurt more when it reveals its emptiness. At the film's gravesite ending, in one of the director's most gorgeous and despairing last shots, Bama finally removes his hat. It's a show of respect, but it's too late. The camera moves past him, capturing a melancholy stone-carved angel and the expanse of the Ohio River beyond, placid, unyielding, and indifferent to the wayward souls upon its shore.

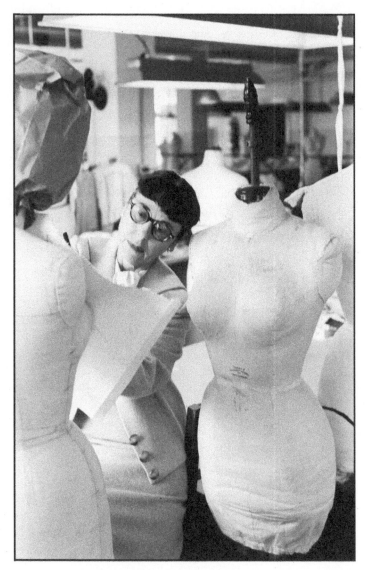
Edith Head at work in her studio, 1959—Inge Morath

ONE FALSE START, NEVER WEAR THE SAME DRESS TWICE

Durga Chew-Bose

T HE MOVIE BEGINS, only to begin a second time, at minute sixteen. She casts a shadow. Like clouds passing over mountains, or in this case, Jimmy Stewart's moonlit sleeping face. Then, we see her: Grace Kelly at her most luminescent, compassed by pearls and the actress's personal patina of something creamy, shiny, like satin, like a painting come to life, a little untouchable. We see her from L.B. "Jeff" Jefferies's perspective (Stewart), and in that glamorous moment, the movie's previous moments—setting up the story of a photojournalist who is recuperating in a wheelchair, restless and entertained by his Greenwich Village neighbors—seemingly evaporate. As the camera pulls away, we dial back. Grace Kelly's entrance as the magazine editor and socialite Lisa Carol Fremont puts forward a clever course correction. In the interest of a dress, Alfred Hitchcock's *Rear Window* (1954) enjoys the good fortune of a false start.

Between minutes sixteen and thirty-two, it's the dress that keeps score. It's the dress that accompanies the duet between Stewart and Kelly's characters, who dance around and debate their relationship's supposed incompatibility (according to Jefferies). It's the dress that delights us as Jefferies drones on about his nomadic life as a photojournalist for magazines like *Life*. It's the dress that duplicates the classic appeal of her red lip. It's the dress that charitably satisfies without sating; layers of white tulle that bloom in contrast to her black V-neck bodice. The dress is more of a sketch than a dress—the purest dream, cinched at the waist, real yet in imagination only. "Right off the Paris plane," she tells Jefferies, furthering the dress's rare-thing extravagance, having only been worn by a special few. In other words, it's the dress's New York debut. A very private debut, which only enhances the spectacle, which only broadens Grace Kelly's kinetic way of providing what only the movies can provide: the ambushing delight of magic—in this case, the dress—and how it familiarizes the audience with the ecstatic.

According to costume designer Edith Head, as noted in Jay Jorgensen's book *Edith Head—The Fifty-Year Career of Hollywood's Greatest Costume Designer*, Hitchcock wanted Kelly to look like "a piece of Dresden china…[He] told me it was important that Grace's clothes help establish some of the conflict in the story." *Rear Window* was the first of four films Head would design for Kelly. They worked closely over the years, dreaming up a style that cared for Kelly's every angle, her potential for glow, and how her characters often possessed an intelligence for transforming an entire scene with the simplest physical gesture, like removing a pair of gloves one finger at a time or reclining in a pistachio-green suit, or swirling snifters of brandy while wearing a sleeveless white dress. Head and Kelly's design relationship seemed to agree on visual details that might fine-tune the story's rhythm, delaying suspense, which ultimately only enhanced it, of course. What is it about wearing a pillbox hat that seems both at odds with and entirely suited to witnessing a man murder his wife?

But back to minute sixteen. The dress—in its own elaborate manner—makes very plain a few truths (and future truths) about the story. While Jefferies is confined to his chair, Lisa Fremont, in contrast, occupies his small apartment with ease and loveliness, gliding more so than taking steps, foreshadowing the nimble nature of her character. Later in the movie, she climbs out of a window and onto a fire escape and Jefferies can only sit and watch helplessly. Hers is a know-how that pays little attention to limitations. She is unconfined in her cinched waist, compelled instead by her compulsive curiosity. She is practiced in arriving and in making exits, and coyly showing little in order to show a lot. The two-tone simplicity, for instance, of her black and white outfit might at first glance appear straightforward in its elegance, but we soon experience its disclosing design. She turns on three lamps and each time, the dress is revealed anew. It frames her clavicles. It greets the length of her satin gloves. And finally, it gives us a show of white chiffon (her shawl) and delicate embroidery (her skirt). "Is this the Lisa Fremont who never wears the same dress twice?" asks Jefferies. "Only because it's expected of her," she responds.

Before leaving Jefferies's apartment, after the couple has argued some more, Lisa says, "I'm in love with you, I don't care what do you do for a living. I'd just like to be part of it somehow." She puts her gloves back on, pushing them up her forearms. She stands by the door, her face half concealed by the night's shadows. She's all dress—the bottom half, white and bright, twirling against her will. She's enchanting. She's heartbroken. As Head said, the clothes were material for establishing conflict. Right. We return to Jefferies, sitting there in his wheelchair. In the wake of her dress, we're left with his pajamas.

MAIGRET
AT THE CORONER'S

EXCERPT

Georges Simenon

'I BET YOU HAVE SOMETHING TO ask me, Julius...'

They were entering the cool interior of an air-conditioned saloon where other gabardine trousers and white shirts and bottles of beer were lined up all along the bar. There were also cowboys, real ones, with their high-heeled boots, broad-brimmed hats and blue jeans tight across their thighs.

'You're right. If we can postpone our visit to Nogales, I'd like to attend the next session of the inquest tomorrow.'

'Cheers! ... No other questions?'

'Lots. I'll ask them as they come to mind. Are there any prostitutes around here?'

'Not in the sense you'd mean. In certain states in America, yes. They're illegal in Arizona.'

'Bessie Mitchell?'

'That's the replacement.'

'Erna Bolton as well?'

'More or less.'

'How many servicemen are on the base?'

'Five or six thousand ... I've never thought about it.'

'Most are unmarried?'

'About three-quarters of them.'

'How do they manage?'

'The best they can. It's not that easy.'

His smile, which rarely left him, was genuine. He certainly respected, perhaps even rather admired Maigret, whom he knew by reputation. Still, it did amuse him to see a Frenchman wrestling with problems so completely foreign to him.

'Myself, I'm from the East,' he announced, not without a touch of pride. 'New England. Here, you see, it's still a little like frontier life. I could have you meet a few old-timers who shot it out with the Apaches at the turn of the century and who sometimes formed an impromptu court to hang a horse or livestock rustler.'

Within the next half-hour they each had three bottles of beer, and Harry Cole reached a decision.

'Whiskey time!'

Later on they drove off in the direction of Nogales; going through Tucson, Maigret was as disconcerted by the city as he had been in the courtroom. With a population of more than a hundred thousand, it was no small town.

And yet, outside the city center and its business district with five or six twenty-story buildings rising into the sky like towers, Tucson looked like a house development—or, rather, like a series of them one beside the other, some richer, others poorer, developments full of trim single-story houses, all equally new.

Further along, streets were no longer paved. For great stretches there was nothing but sand and a few cacti. They drove past the airport, and suddenly the desert was everywhere, with the mountains violet in the distance.

'Here is about where it happened. Do you want to get out? Keep an eye open for rattlesnakes.'

'Are there any?'

'Sometimes they turn up even in the city.'

The railway tracks were a single line running about fifty yards from the highway.

'I think there are four or five trains every twenty-four hours. Sure you don't want to go and have a drink in Mexico? Nogales is right nearby.'

Sixty miles away! In the end, however, they drove there in less than an hour.

A small town with a fence cutting across the two main streets. Men in uniforms. Harry Cole spoke to them and a moment later he was plunging with Julius into a sudden bustle of people on narrow, littered streets bathed in a surprising bronze glow.

'We'll start at the Caves Bar, even though it is a mite too early.'

Half-naked urchins pestered them, eager to shine their shoes, and shopkeepers tried to detain them at the threshold of every souvenir store.

'As you can see, it's a carnival. When folks from Tucson or even Phoenix or farther away want to have fun, they come here.'

In the immense bar, they really did see nothing but Americans.

'You think Bessie Mitchell was killed?' asked Maigret.

'All I know is that she's dead.'

'Accidentally?'

'I have to say that it has nothing to do with me: it isn't a federal crime, and I deal only with them. Everything else is taken care of by the county police.'

In other words, the sheriff and his deputies. That was really what most bewildered Maigret, much more than the baroque and odorous funfair into which he had plunged.

In charge of the county police, the sheriff was in no way a public servant promoted through the ranks or by examinations, but a citizen elected much as a municipal councilor was in Paris. His previous occupation was of no importance. He put himself forward as a candidate and campaigned for the job.

Once elected, he chose his own deputies—his 'inspectors'—as he pleased: the fellows Maigret had seen with big revolvers and cartridge-studded belts.

'That's not all!' added Harry Cole with a touch of irony. 'Besides the appointed deputy sheriffs, there are all the others…'

'Like me?' joked Maigret, thinking of the silver badge he had received.

'I'm talking about the sheriff's friends, influential in his election, who get the same badge. For example, just about every rancher is a deputy sheriff. Don't think they take this lightly. A few weeks ago, a car stolen by a dangerous escaped convict was traveling between Tucson and Nogales. The sheriff of Tucson alerted a rancher who lives about halfway along that route and who then called two or three neighbors, livestock ranchers like himself. They were all deputy sheriffs. They set up a roadblock with their vehicles, and when the stolen car attempted to get past, they shot out its tires, then made a show of firing at the driver, whom they wound up capturing with a lasso. What do you think of that?'

Maigret had not yet had as many drinks as the witnesses on the stand had put away, but it was beginning to tell on him, and he muttered with some difficulty, 'In France, the locals would have tried to stop the police instead.'

He was not sure exactly when they got back to Tucson…

Translated by Linda Coverdale

SUNBELT NOIR:
DESERT FURY

Imogen Sara Smith

A LONG, STRAIGHT ROAD slices through the emptiness of the desert, under a sky piled with towering mesas of cloud. A speck appears in the distance and swells into a sleek gray Chrysler, carrying two men in grey suits—part of the migration of East Coast mobsters sweeping into Las Vegas. This is how *Desert Fury* (1947) opens, in a modern West thoroughly tainted by crime, corruption, and social snobbery, just as the landscape is marred by smokestacks, pylons, and oil wells. Much of the film looks like a glossy brochure for a high-end Southwest resort, aglow with burnished golds and sandstone reds; the immaculately chic denizens, posed against backdrops of spiky cactus and sculpted rock formations, never show a smudge of dirt of a blotch of sweat. They flock to the Purple Sage Saloon & Casino to enjoy a fantasy of rip-roaring wild-west debauchery, pouring their money into the pockets of vice queen Fritzi Haller (Mary Astor). "The wages of sin," she gloats, "are very high."

Lewis Allen's *Desert Fury* combines elements of film noir, melodrama, and the western, fusing them in a blaze of Technicolor and outrageously overheated emotional warfare. The film richly deserves its cult status as one of the queerest products of studio-era Hollywood, but its campy reputation obscures the sharpness of its underlying themes. The rodeo, often talked about but never witnessed, symbolizes the way all of the film's relationships are contests for dominance, filled with brazen assertions of control and humiliating gestures of submission. The plot is constructed as an interlocking set of love triangles, all anchored by the trophy blonde Paula Haller (Lizabeth Scott) and the mysterious racketeer Eddie Bendix (John Hodiak), whose paths cross in the opening scene as both motor into the Nevada town of Chuckawalla.

Paula's mother Fritzi runs the town, treating the sheriff as her lapdog. She can buy her daughter everything except respectability, and the rebellious girl bounces out of every finishing school she's sent to. She chafes at her mother's domineering, possessive love, but is excited by the brutish way Eddie orders people around. Tom Hanson (Burt Lancaster), the virile, clean-cut deputy sheriff who loves Paula, thinks Eddie killed his own wife years earlier in a road accident on the edge of town. Eddie's ever-present companion Johnny (Wendell Corey) is so fanatically jealous that he threatens to kill Paula if she doesn't stay away from them. The more she is warned against Eddie, the more stubbornly Paula pursues the forbidden affair, leading to an escalating series of confrontations, face-slappings, scheming, and gloriously bad behavior. The affable, straight-arrow Hanson abuses his police power to arrest and beat up his rival, who regresses into the scared street punk he obviously once was. Fritzi offends Hanson's male pride by trying to bribe him into marrying Paula. A former rodeo rider, now "all busted up inside," Hanson tells Paula that what she's looking for in life is the thrill he got in the ring—of being alone, on top, the champ. He's still addicted to breaking horses, and sees his would-be bride as a filly who should be given a long rope.

Desert Fury was produced by Hal Wallis, who headed an independent unit at Paramount and assembled his own stock company of actors. Among his finds were Lancaster, Corey, and Scott, a husky-voiced siren—unglamorously born Emma Matzo in Scranton, Pennsylvania—for whom Wallis nursed a consuming, lifelong obsession. She was always a bit stiff on screen, but her radiance in Technicolor—proving that "spun-gold" hair is not just the hyperbole of fairy tales—fully justifies the tug-of-war she inspires in this story. But the film belongs to Mary Astor. Only forty-one, she had already been slotted into sweet, mother-hen roles, and she relished the chance to play the steely, neurotic Fritzi Haller: "I could use all my accumulated bitterness and bad temper and do a little exploding." Fritzi's overbearing attachment to her daughter seems more than maternal: in their first scene she greets her with, "You look good, baby, give me a kiss." Later, during a thunderstorm, she offers to sleep with Paula, recalling how the girl used to come into her bed when she was frightened by thunder. Astor seems to encourage this coding with her slacks and close-cropped hairdo, her brusque, authoritative manner. She also suggests a woman whose harsh life—Fritzi came up through the silk mills of Paterson, New Jersey, and married a bootlegger—has made her tough but also insecure, with deep wells of anger and cynicism.

The other most interesting character is Fritzi's counterpart, Johnny, whom Wendell Corey makes both pitiful and menacing, with his lifeless voice and pale, frozen eyes. The two men have been together "for a long, long time," ever since Johnny picked up the teenaged Eddie in Times Square when he was broke and homeless. Now, Johnny keeps house and waits on Eddie as he sunbathes bare-chested; Eddie barks orders at Johnny, nastily belittling him and slapping his face just as Fritzi slaps Paula's. The sinister, subservient Johnny insists that Eddie will never leave him because "I come in too handy," while Fritzi assures herself that she'll never lose her daughter because "she needs me." It's hard to fathom how the implications of the men's living arrangements flew under the gaydars of the Breen Office censors, but in any case their inseparable, co-dependent relationship is far more complex than a mere souring romance. Linked by a shared history of crime and violence, the two gangsters are really one: Eddie is an empty shell with the looks and charisma the world expects of a tough guy; the nondescript Johnny is the brains, the guts, and the will behind him. In the end, rejected by the front man he has propped up and manipulated, Johnny has an epiphany: "People think they're seeing Eddie, and all the time they're seeing me. *I'm* Eddie Bendix."

This snarled web of relationships has deep roots, burrowing into a swamp of murky secrets—the death of Eddie's wife, who looked just like Paula; Fritzi's history with Eddie back East—and as in any film noir, the past throws long shadows over the present. But the look of the film, awash in sunlight and warm colors, banishes the moody chiaroscuro you expect from noir. Edith Head's designs for Paula and Fritzi are a harmony of ochres and brick reds and creams and forest greens, with eye-popping touches of chartreuse and hot pink. (Head grew up in the Southwest, living for a time in Searchlight, Nevada, and her taste for Mexican and western-wear touches, along with her preference for sporty, clean-lined clothes for modern women, are on full display here.) Paula's car, a wood-paneled, burgundy 1946 Chrysler, matches the bougainvillea that smothers the porch of the Haller mansion, a Victorian fantasia with ovoid windows, ornate plasterwork, and a battlemented stone turret. (The Piru Mansion in Ventura County, California was used for exteriors; parts of *Desert Fury* were also filmed in Cottonwood and other Nevada locations.) The lavish interiors built in the studio incorporate the house's eye-shaped windows, framing weirdly lit mesas, and feature lush plants, pink carpets, and moss-green sofas.

A tryst between Eddie and Paula is bathed in syrupy orange firelight that seems to parody the cloying, romance-novel prose she reads aloud. The cinematography by Charles Lang recalls Leon Shamroy's for the quintessential noir-in-color, John M. Stahl's *Leave Her to Heaven* (1945), which opens in a luxurious desert hideaway. Both these films exploit Technicolor's unnatural, saturated hues and the airless perfection of Hollywood's magazine-spread vision of the good life. They are feverish melodramas enacted in a strangely frozen, sleepwalking style, and both seduce the eye with luscious beauty while telling ugly stories, creating an unsettling dissonance.

Paula likes "to be alone in the desert, with the sagebrush and the sky," but to Eddie, Nevada is a "cactus graveyard," recalling the way Chuck Tatum (Kirk Douglas), the exiled New York newspaperman in Billy Wilder's *Ace in the Hole* (1951), sneers at New Mexico as "this sun-baked Siberia." On the surface, *Desert Fury* presents the West as a pure, wholesome land invaded and polluted by Eastern vices, but it subtly undermines Western myths. The mountains and rock formations that ring the horizon give the landscape a closed-in feel. The long straight road that should represent freedom and escape seems to lead nowhere, as if its vanishing point in the distance were no optical illusion. In *Film Comment*, critic Ronald Bergen quipped, "There is almost as much driving with people getting nowhere in *Desert Fury* as in an Abbas Kiarostami movie." People are always jumping in cars and roaring off, but winding up back where they started.

This motif can no doubt be traced to notorious car-nut A.I. "Buzz" Bezzerides, who co-wrote the screenplay with Robert Rossen, from the novel *Desert Town* by Ramona Stewart. Vehicles as death traps or murder weapons, a recurring theme that would reach its fullest expression in Bezzerides' script for *Kiss Me Deadly* (1955), appears here, and so at the end does the transient, banal, melancholy world of roadside diners where people stop for cigarettes and hamburgers on their way to nowhere.

The postwar expansion of interstate highways and suburbs, and the explosion of growth in California and the Southwest, gave rise to Sunbelt Noir. The 1950s saw a sudden spate of films set in the desert, exploiting the glamour of mid-century playgrounds and the dusty solitude of last-chance gas stations, motels, and abandoned boomtowns. The desert was a cheap, potent location for Poverty Row quickies like *Highway Dragnet* (1954) and *The Scarf* (1951); an allegorical setting for the portraits of an arid, callously extractive society in *Ace in the Hole* and *The Prowler* (1953). *The Tattered Dress* (1957) offers a prescient take on the clash between wealthy coastal newcomers and locals whose resentment curdles into anti-elitist, proto-MAGA hate. In *Violent Saturday* (1955), a hot-hued Technicolor soap opera set in a town so rife with lurid secrets that a trio of visiting bank robbers seem more well-adjusted than the locals, the open wound of a strip mine represents industrial America's original sin against the land. *Split Second* (1953) brings a gang of escaped convicts and their hostages to a ghost town during the countdown to an atomic bomb test. The threat of nuclear annihilation hangs over the desert like a shadow out of a cloudless sky.

Desert Fury also looks ahead to other films about the modern West, like *The Lusty Men* (1952), *The Misfits* (1961), and *Lonely Are the Brave* (1962). All these films were the products of left-wing writers—like Rossen and Bezzerides—who seem torn between boyish, romantic idealization of the cowboy as a symbol of rugged individualism, and mournful disillusionment about the degraded reality behind the myth. Film noir and the western may seem worlds apart, but they share similar misgivings about American ideals: a fixation with the corrosive power of money and greed; a sense of the elusiveness, and illusoriness, of freedom in a society predicated on it; a haunting alienation and isolation. "A guy's alone," Eddie Bendix explains. "All his life he's alone. He keeps trying not to be alone."

The darkness buried at the heart of the western is its tendency to see freedom not as a universal right or a communal value, but as a finite resource to be fought over, like land or oil or gold. For someone to win the rodeo, someone else must be broken. Paula reaches the end of her long rope, and seals her surrender by kissing her mother on the lips. In a final scene shot day-for-night, she and Tom Hanson gaze out over a vista anchored by looming black smokestacks, then walk off towards the walled horizon in the uncanny, shaded brightness that the French aptly call "the American night." No one achieves the fantasy of independence, "to be alone in the desert, with the sagebrush and the sky."

THE VOYAGE DOWN
AND OUT: *INFERNO*

Kent Jones

I T'S REWARDING to look at *Inferno* (1953), 20th Century
Fox's one and only 3-D production, in the company of other
Robinson Crusoe narratives, in which the hero finds himself in
a situation where he has no choice but to use his own ingenuity
and intelligence in order to survive and eventually escape. As
Robert Ryan's pampered millionaire with a busted leg, left to
die in the Mojave Desert by his wife (Rhonda Fleming) and
his mining engineer (William Lundigan), builds his own splint
and lowers himself from a rocky ledge to the desert floor with
braided canvas rope, you might see parallels with *A Man Escaped*.
When he uses his jackknife to cut open a barrel cactus to suck
moisture from the pulp, or when he digs through layers and
layers of sand to get to the water underground, anyone who
remembers the Canadian kids' classic *My Side of the Mountain*
will see the kinship. When he sprawls in a little patch of shade,
sun parched, trying to save his energy to simply go on, *The Flight
of the Phoenix* will probably come to mind.

In each of these titles and others sprinkled throughout film
history (*Lifeboat, Island in the Sky, Escape from Alcatraz, Le Trou,
Walkabout, Castaway,* Dave's perilous return to the spacecraft

in *2001*, *Apollo 13*, the opening stretch of *There Will Be Blood*), everything is boiled down to immediate physical reality. We zero in on the action, the effort and the basic know-how needed to create rope from bed springs and a shredded blanket, to construct a new plane from the ruins of an old one, to scale a craggy rock face with a broken leg. Questions of food and water, light and darkness, heat and cold become momentous.

Until its incendiary climax, which involves a little too much convoluted spatial and dramatic maneuvering, *Inferno* is bracingly and refreshingly elemental. We start with a warning sign in the middle of the desert: "Do not attempt this route without ample supplies of water-gas-oil." A man, Lundigan, takes big deliberate steps as a beautiful woman dressed in dude ranch finery, Fleming, nervously watches; he throws empty whiskey bottles along his path; he gets into a station wagon attached to an empty horse trailer and drives it into the dirt. The pieces of a diversionary scenario are being put in place. They mount the horses and the first lines are spoken. "It's not like killing him... exactly," says Fleming, "more just not saving him." "It's killing him alright," answers Lundigan. We stay with this joyless couple for six minutes before we get to Ryan, shooting with a revolver at an empty whiskey bottle while he swigs from another one, and screaming at the sky. "Where are they?!?"

There are no emotional curlicues or supplementary plots to follow. Everything is strictly functional, and that includes the people. As a "couple," Lundigan and Fleming are the definition of shallow. Their romance is three nights old, and leaving Ryan in the canyon is a spur-of-the-moment inspiration. As they playact the details of their tale, they're both sized up, dryly and efficiently, by Ryan's lawyer (Larry Keating) and the local sheriff and his deputy. The lawyer also does a good job of sizing up Ryan, once the odds of his survival have slimmed: "If he hadn't grown up with so much money in a world where it has such power, he might have been quite a guy."

The Lundigan, Fleming and Keating characters exist in the film to generate suspense (how long before everyone realizes that Ryan's character has made it out of the canyon, and what will they do?) and to provide a series of extra-dry, mordant contrasts to the desperate situation of Ryan's Donald Whitney Carson III. A parched and starving Carson takes a shot at a mourning dove and misses—cut to Lundigan diving into a pool and swimming to Fleming, decorously but worriedly sunbathing in a gold lamé swimsuit, before Keating approaches in a complementary gold and white checked robe. Carson digs with a rock for water—cut to Lundigan fixing a lemon soda. Every composition in these creature comfort hinge scenes is carefully wrought in complementary shades of sky blue, aqua marine and desert tan, creating a maximum concentration of leisure and ease in a minimum of set-ups to offset the core drama in the desert.

The comfortably set individual forced onto a morally and physically level playing field is crucial to the Crusoe narrative, and to films like the aforementioned *Castaway* or the Lee Tamahori/David Mamet *The Edge* (and *The Crew*, a long-gestating and beloved project of Michelangelo Antonioni's that sadly went unmade). And what makes *Inferno* so special is the conviction brought to the drama of man and nature, each equally present and vivid. It's the right actor in the right desert, guided by the right director (Roy Ward Baker) flanked by the right DP (Lucien Ballard, who shot Baker's earlier *Don't Bother to Knock* and would go on to work with Boetticher, Kubrick and, famously, Peckinpah), working from a tight, inspired script by Francis Cockrell. And let's also say a word for Don Greenwood, a veteran prop man who entered the business in 1925 at the suggestion of Raoul Walsh and who worked on over 100 films and TV series, mostly without credit, through the mid-sixties. Carson's leather pouch and the protective mitts he fashions from its flap cover, his improvised crutch and splint, his dusty green bed roll... if you find yourself remarking on the rightness of those items and others, think of the uncredited Mr. Greenwood.

Greenwood brings professionalism. Cockrell does the same, with a gift for irony. Ballard brings a real feeling for natural southwestern light (and that one indispensable tool common to all great DPs, a mind for geometry). Baker, who worked as a second AD in England under Hitchcock (on *The Lady Vanishes*) and Carol Reed, brings a dry touch, a terrific sense of visual and narrative economy and a careful attention to detail. But Robert Ryan and the Mojave Desert... that's magic.

Inferno was shot in the southwestern portion of the Mojave— Joshua Tree country. The gnarled, haunted forms of those yucca plants that grow like trees (given its now more famous name by the Mormons for Joshua's outstretched arms, once known to the Spanish as Dagger of the Desert) rhyme visually with the equally gnarled and haunted face of Ryan himself, and the expanse and topographical complexity of this particular desert harmonizes with the length and power of his body. Ryan, one of the finest and most creative actors in the history of movies, was a triple threat: he moved beautifully, he spoke expressively, and he was brilliant—there are many moments in his films where his own mining of values embedded in the material visibly surpasses that of the director.

The actor thought that this was one of his finest performances, and the actor was right. Apart from an excessively athletic showdown with Lundigan near the end (mostly fought by stuntmen), there's not one wrong note. The details of Carson's boredom and despair, his dawning realization that he's been abandoned, his determination to make it out, his meticulous preparations, his slow and perilous descent and his ongoing maintenance of his own energies as he searches for food and water—every stage in his trek out of the canyon and in his growing consciousness of himself as an able man is given its full measure. Sometimes, it's a matter of the visualization of a given event, as with Carson's initial descent. Whenever one director has worked for another director early in his or her career, it's tempting to cite the "influence." But for Baker, working on *The Lady Vanishes* really was, as he himself said, "a great education." He sets up the height from which Carson must descend and the tricky terrain he must negotiate with a level of patience, care and clarity that Hitchcock would have applauded. In one especially breathtaking shot, the camera pivots to an overhead angle on Ryan's double as Carson starts the hair-raising descent—a vertiginously beautiful image, particularly in 3-D.

At other moments, Ryan is the one who makes the scene work. Before he can build his splint, Carson realizes that he'll have to set his own leg. Ryan shimmies his big body over to two adjoining boulders in which he can wedge the leg with a believable awkwardness and hesitation. "This won't be jolly," he dryly exclaims in the running voiceover. He braces himself, sets back slowly as he tries to psych himself up, and... In an early fifties Hollywood movie, the details of an actual improvised bone-setting were off-limits. When Carson pulls the leg together, Baker cuts to a close-up of Ryan's reaction that transmits a pretty fair portion of the surge of pain. When Carson is digging for water, the pattern is two repeated set-ups: tight on Ryan's face and shoulders as he digs, tight on his hand shoveling the dirt back in the hole. The appearance of pooling water comes too quickly (out of necessity, it's a manufactured event), but Ryan's voiceover makes it work. Before the scene is broken in two by the cut to Lundigan drinking the lemon soda, Ryan fantasizes about the water that will come pouring down from the mountains come spring. There's a beautifully executed pan down a red rockface and over a steep little path down. "In the spring, when the snow melts up above, it will wash everything away," muses Carson to himself. "This will be a waterfall, and a big pool." The sense of wonder tinged with longing builds in his voice, edging into an imagined slaking of thirst: "It will make a lot of roar... and splash... and mist..." And as he rhapsodizes ("Must remember: always visit the desert in the spring..."), it dawns on him that he's sitting in the middle of a basin that's dry only on the top layer, and he starts digging. "If it would only stop falling back in..." And then: "I smell it... I smell it! Isn't that fantastic?" The language is good, but Ryan lifts it to the realm of music—great, jubilatory, sinewy American music, all of a piece with his expressive body language. I don't think any other actor could have articulated every mood and surge of feeling as beautifully as Ryan does here with Baker—together, they make Carson's renewal and transformation into a cinematic event, every movement and shift in vocal timbre tied to the excitingly varied desert terrain.

Inferno is ultimately a pulp construction, and Ryan's meeting with Henry Hull's lone prospector and his big confrontation with Lundigan in Hull's desert shack, while nicely executed, both seem more inevitable to the genre than to what is best in the film. But the very end of *Inferno*—Ryan and Hull find a disheveled Fleming wandering down the highway and Ryan invites her aboard Hull's homemade all-terrain vehicle—is a thing of beauty. No vengeance, no tears. Just a reborn man at peace with himself, his would-be murdering wife who always figured it would end this way, and the interested party behind the wheel, going down the road in silence.

BAD DAY NEAR
THE RIVER'S EDGE

Nicolas Saada

WHEN WES ASKED ME to write about a film, I naturally replied, "I'll choose two." What do a realistic, edgy John Sturges thriller and an Allan Dwan melodrama have in common? "*Nothing*," would be the answer. And yet, something has always intrigued me about both films.

First of all, I love CinemaScope, with its slight image distortions, and a particular cutting style that the format seems to impose. Then, there is the setting: both titles are film noirs that take place far from the cities, in a landscape familiar to the western: the desert, the open country, the woods.

These two films feature actors that I have always considered to be part of a "dangerous cinema"; big stars, but whose faces have also been seen in obscure American films little known to the general public. In *Bad Day at Black Rock* (1955), you have Spencer Tracy; in sharp opposition to him, there is a gallery of wicked villains from the great B-movies of the period: Lee Marvin, Ernest Borgnine and, last but not least, Robert Ryan, who to my knowledge, never made a bad movie. In *The River's Edge* (1957), Ray Milland is as suave and unsettling as ever, just like in the films he made with Fritz Lang or John Farrow. When

Ray Milland is around, there is a promise of intrigue, deceit, double-dealing, and murder.

In the end, these films deal with the theme of the intruder, but they differ in the way they handle the subject. In *Bad Day at Black Rock*, the intruder is the embodiment of Good in a community plagued by Evil. In *The River's Edge*, Evil is the intruder that disrupts the lives of a pair of good characters as they try to make a new start. In both cases, the intruder brings with him chaos, uncertainty, violence. I wouldn't claim the films are similar: I leave that kind of analysis to another film writer. Yet, I believe that films have an almost organic life of their own, and that they illuminate each other like paintings hung side by side on a museum wall. That's my slightly *flâneur* approach to cinema.

One cannot imagine a ratio other than CinemaScope for *Bad Day at Black Rock*. The film opens with a train speeding through a desert landscape—a black line on a plain background—the use of widescreen all the more appropriate, like an abstract expressionist painting. André Prévin's menacing music rings out; violence speeds across the desert. Spencer Tracy's ominous arrival could be compared to Joseph Cotten's in Alfred Hitchcock's *Shadow of a Doubt* (1943). A train pulling into a small city is never good news. However, in Sturges's film, the train doesn't even stop in a small city. The buildings look more like miniature stations for electric toy trains, with hardly any houses. That's the brilliance of the film: you have a sparse plot, in a minimalist setting, that pits hyper-powerful, acutely drawn characters against each other; the contrast between the strong personality of all these people, and the starkness of their environment. *Bad Day at Black Rock* can best be described by the word tension: from the first frames it never stops. We see a resolute hero, who is searching for the truth, facing a frightened community that is kept under the rule of silence. The central visual idea of the film is to make Spencer Tracy a man in black, moving in space, impossible to avoid, impossible to disappear. Everybody notices him, no matter where he goes. That's great.

What inspired Sturges? John Ford, no doubt, but also Italian neorealism, and classic Japanese cinema. As a Hollywood director of the period, he would have seen them all. I love his early noirs, *Mystery Street* (1950) or *The People Against O'Hara* (1951). He also remade *Seven Samurai* (1954), as *The Magnificent Seven* (1960), a few years before the outbreak of the spaghetti in Europe. Shrewd, he was. I can't stand the phrase "less is more," but, in the case of *Bad Day at Black Rock*, less has never been more. It's an ascetic action film.

The River's Edge was made two years after *Bad Day at Black Rock*, and shares with Sturges's film a very sparse setting and a complex, disturbing plot. We are never sure of the period in which the film unfolds. If Sturges's film is set in a kind of high realism, with its unity of time and place, Dwan's is more poetic, and even sometimes a bit abstract. It starts out like a screwball comedy, complete with all the classic ingredients—a married couple in a state of crisis with scenes that remind us of Leo McCarey—and these narrative elements are soon nuanced by the scenery, suggesting a western.

Dwan started out as a director in the silent era, and you only need to watch a few shots of the films he made in the 1910s to realize that he was already a visual poet. Dwan is a filmmaker who seems closer to Raoul Walsh than Anthony Mann, and I am constantly amazed by the vulnerability of his characters; a vulnerability that leaves each scene always on the edge, in balance, with no indication of which direction it will take. *The River's Edge* has one of the most beautiful sequences in cinema history: the murder of a patrolman on a country road, and then a car and foot chase through open fields. The shots, the framing, the use of day for night are unforgettable. This is the best Douglas Sirk scene not directed by Douglas Sirk.

The film is a story of a *ménage à trois*, about a woman caught between a man she is trying to love, a strong and honest farmer (Anthony Quinn), the man she is trying to forget, a manipulative crook (Ray Milland), and the physical, emotional journey of this central female character, the great Debra Paget. Dwan has equal empathy for all the characters, but he still has a moral worldview that you can feel in every shot of the film. Quinn has seldom been so great, despite a character that might have been unappealing if played by another actor.

Dwan's film is not in the minimalist vein of Sturges, yet I could say he's a kind of stripped-down baroque: every plot twist in *The River's Edge* is extreme, but the handling is always understated and cool. Every time I watch *Bad Day at Black Rock* and *The River's Edge* I enjoy and study the style, but still I am on the edge of my seat. Maybe that's why I associate these films in my mind. Something brings them together, holds them together, like two false twins of 1950s American cinema.

Oddly enough, I never had the opportunity to discuss these two films with Wes Anderson, with whom I often have long conversations about movies. With the publication of this piece, my hope is that it will provide us all with the encouragement to see and talk about these two profoundly stimulating and original films.

"All the News
That's Fit to Print"

The New York Times.

LATE CITY EDITION
Mostly sunny today; cooler to-
night. Fair tomorrow.
Temperature Range Today—Max., 61; Min., 49
Temperature Yesterday—Max., 64; Min., 48
Full U. S. Weather Bureau Report, Page 47

Copyright, 1952, by The New York Times Company.

VOL. CI..No. 34,632.   NEW YORK, FRIDAY, MAY 2, 1952.   FIVE CENTS

Marines Get Taste Of Atomic Warfare

By GLADWIN HILL
Special to THE NEW YORK TIMES.

LAS VEGAS, Nev., May 1— About 2,100 men engaged in the first Marine Corps atomic warfare maneuvers today as the Atomic Energy Commission set off another atomic bomb at its Nevada proving ground, the twenty-eighth bomb exploded by this country.

The troops, crouched in foxholes three to four miles from "ground zero," the point directly under the explosion, probably were closer to a nuclear blast than any large group in history, with the exception of the Japanese who experienced the World War II atomic attacks.

This indicated that within the space of ten days our knowledge of the employment of atomic bombs as tactical weapons has been pushed substantially forward.

The bomb, dropped from an Air Force plane over Yucca Flat, was about the same size as the one detonated April 22 in a similar pioneering exercise with Army troops as participants. A view of the explosion from 11,000-foot Mount Charleston, 50 miles away, provided the estimate of the size of the bomb.

Altitude Markedly Lower

Today's bomb was exploded at a markedly lower altitude—probably about 2,000 feet, in contrast to last week's altitude of 3,000 to 3,500 feet.

This and other important alterations in the elements of the test— not perceptible in the explosion's central "fireball"—were hinted in the renewed exclusion from the proving ground of the members of the press, some 200 of whom were allowed to watch last week's explosion at close range. Official secrecy was maintained about the altitude of today's explosion, in contrast to last week's explicit announcement.

The lower altitude was attested in the behavior of the blast. Last week's explosion was so high that it failed to suck up a solid column of dust linking the atomic cloud with the ground.

Today such a column, grayolack, massive and dense, surged up instantly and persisted as a solid "stalk" for many minutes. The rolling, red-orange "fireball" following the initial flash was visible for the unusually long period of ten seconds, and the cottony white radioactive cloud that developed soared quickly to four or five miles before it was caught by the wind and attenuated southward.

Test Progress Manifest

What the armed forces are anxious to arrive at is an atomic explosion low enough to do maximum damage to an enemy position and at the same time high enough to protect our near-by forces, poised for an advance, and obviate persisting ground radioactivity which would delay such an advance.

Today's experiment manifestly brought the two sides of the compromise a little closer together.

Immediately after the explosion, according to official reports, the marines jumped out of the same five-foot-deep foxholes and trenches used by the Army last week and, as the explosion area was pronounced safe by radiological safety teams, moved forward in vehicles to "ground zero."

The marines, organized in two provisional battalions, were a cross-section of corps personnel drawn from eastern and western bases and stations as far away as Hawaii with the idea that they would return to their units and relay their experiences.

MARINES CHARGING AFTER ATOM BLAST

Troopers moving on an "objective" seconds after explosion during tactical exercises at the Nevada proving grounds northeast of Las Vegas yesterday.

'The Atomic City,' Low-Budget, High-Voltage Paramount Film, Opens at the Mayfair

THE ATOMIC CITY, written by Sydney Boehm; directed by Jerry Hopper; produced by Joseph Sistrom for Paramount Pictures. At the Mayfair.

Dr. Frank Addison	Gene Barry
Martha Addison	Lydia Clarke
Tommy Addison	Lee Aaker
Russ Farley	Michael Moore
Ellen Haskell	Nancy Gates
Peggy Marston	Bonny Kay Eddy
Gregory	Housely Stevenson Jr.
Inspector Mann	Milburn Stone
Weinberg	Frank Cady
Driscoll	Norman Budd
Donald Clark	Leonard Strong
Jablons	Bert Freed
Arnie Molter	Anthony Ward
Peter Rassett	John Damler
Robert Kalnick	George M. Lynn

By BOSLEY CROWTHER

Paramount has got a "sleeper" —a low-budget, high-voltage film —in its new "The Atomic City," which came to the Mayfair yesterday. Streamlined and realistic in its feverish telling of a tale of the rescue of a small son of a Los Alamos physicist who has been kidnapped by H-bomb spies, this trim little piece of melodrama wastes no time on solemn messages. It is made for suspense and excitement, and those are what it gives. Directed by Jerry Hopper, a young man who has previously done only Army training films and documentaries, it introduces a talent to be watched.

In two respects, Mr. Hopper was fortunate, indeed. He had a script of considerable potential, written by Sydney Boehm. He also had the advantage of shooting almost the whole film in the actual locations specified in New Mexico and Los Angeles. Thus the high-powered, electrifying aura of the Los Alamos atom plant, where the story begins, is generated with the authority of a documentary film. The trailing of a kidnapping suspect through the streets of Los Angeles and in the local ballpark becomes as vivid as a running news photograph. And the ultimate heart-in-throat round-up of the murderous kidnapper-spies on a high Indian pueblo and cliff-dwelling is as "visual" as a trip to Santa Fé.

Along with this pictorial sharpness, Mr. Hopper has kept the tale of personal and police anxiety at

Lee Aaker in "The Atomic City"

a point of desperation all the way. From the moment the physicist's youngster is suddenly discovered missing while his school class is on a visit to a fiesta in Santa Fé, the tension is that of a bowstring. And, despite certain holes in the plot, the pace is so fast and precipitous that you'll not likely notice the bumps. The final rescue of the youngster from a cliff is as breathless as such can be.

In a cast made up largely of unknowns, Gene Barry does a fine, authentic job as the Los Alamos atom-juggler and Milburn Stone is collected and cool as the chief of the F. B. I. army assigned to nab the spies. Lydia Clarke as the scientist's wife and the boy's mother, Michael Moore as one of the sleuths and Nancy Gates, Norman Budd and several others are good in supporting roles.

But it is a tow-headed youngster named Lee Aaker who runs away with the show—at the end, at least, when he is struggling to escape from the kidnapping spies. If this little fellow doesn't pull you right off the edge of your chair, which is where you should most of the time be sitting, then we'll miss our guess about this film.

WATCHING *FAIL SAFE* AT
THE END OF THE WORLD

K. Austin Collins

"THIS IS THE PRESIDENT of the United States." It's a line
that makes intrinsic sense when it comes from the mouth
of Henry Fonda—a paragon of world-weary Hollywood integ-
rity if ever there were one. In Sidney Lumet's *Fail Safe* (1964),
Fonda declares "I am the president" with the authority of a man
whose face is already immortalized on our national currency.
Watching Lumet's film, however, you quickly grow to wish you
were hearing it under better circumstances.

The time is the paranoid '60s, during the long political tail of
the Cuban Missile Crisis. The place: a constellation of government and military offices in the United States, ranging from
Fonda's post in an underground bunker to caverns of the U.S.
Strategic Air Command at Offutt Air Force Base in Omaha,
Nebraska to the cockpit of a "Vindicator" bomber—the source
of all the movie's trouble. The mood, predictably, is panic.

Lumet, best known for films like *12 Angry Men*, *Dog Day
Afternoon*, and *Network*, has a knack for landing a tight, winning
premise. *Fail Safe*, a box office failure in its time that's been
considered a classic ever since, is no exception. The stakes
couldn't be higher: a thermonuclear first strike by the U.S. on

the Soviet Union has accidentally, or perhaps inevitably, been set into motion. Moscow is about to be obliterated, which of course portends a Soviet counterstrike, which further portends an all-out nuclear holocaust.

It's a premise beset with irony. In a way, things go as wrong as they do because the men fated to carry out this mission are good soldiers: they cannot be deterred. The U.S.'s military strategy is *so* well-honed and carefully planned, so prepared to set the vehicle of war into motion, that as they near their targets, the Vindicator bombers are trained not to trust any orders to abort their mission—not even from their own president. Because, you see, the voice of the president can be imitated. The Americans have thought of everything.

Everything, that is, but their own failure. *Fail Safe* is based on a bestselling 1962 novel of the same name by Eugene Burdick and Harvey Wheeler, which had been serialized *during* the Cuban Missile Crisis in the *Saturday Evening Post*. It was fiction, not journalism, but that made it no less terrifying. And its adaptation to the screen by Walter Bernstein—a writer who'd been blacklisted by the studio system during the McCarthy witch hunts—has the added heft of an exile's skepticism. The film is, among other things, a riveting critique of boys and their toys—the boys being the people pulling the strings of these world powers, and the toys being weapons of nuclear annihilation.

Rewatching it recently—spurred, maybe, by an urge to escape our own crisis by vicariously panicking through someone else's—I got an eerie feeling. Nuclear wars and pandemics aren't analogous. But they do share a penchant for wiping people out, speeding along to worst-case scenarios while our heaving, indecisive bureaucratic structures trail them in the rear view. Like any other international crisis, they both depend on powerful people in rooms making decisions on behalf of the rest of humanity. Relatedly, they also depend on the public's implicit trust in those powers.

Which is but one reason that *Fail Safe*'s near-absence of a "public" makes it so intense. With "us," the audience, removed from the action—with almost no one on screen meant to approximate the average American, suffering laws rather than making them—we become all the more beholden to the incumbent tragedy. We imagine ourselves "out there" in the dramatic negative space of the movie, living our lives, completely unaware as a violent disruption—perhaps the end of society as we know it—looms invisibly over our heads.

It's no wonder Lumet makes some of the formal choices he makes here—an absence of music, for example, which makes the entire film not only quiet enough for a guy to hear himself think, but quiet enough to those most panicked, most paranoid thoughts upon him. It's also no wonder that we get a real voice of anti-reason coursing through the film, a political scientist played by Walter Matthau and unabashedly inspired by the physicist and futurist Herman Kahn, who once asked us to think the unthinkable.

Matthau's confident but ultimately, in the heat of a real conflict, unpersuasive professor spends most of the film in the Pentagon, among the president's closest advisers. From the moment we meet him, it is clear this is a bad idea. This is a man who weighs the toll of nuclear war in relative terms. For him, winning means that American *civilization* will at least have a chance of surviving, even if millions of Americans do not. His ability to neatly parse these things—civilization, citizens—sums him up. And the movie. Somehow, without even showing us the public whose lives are at stake, Lumet forces you to imagine the real, material consequences of what, in Matthau's mouth, feels like an abstract game of numbers.

That's what *Fail Safe* reveals war to be about—even as the people onscreen seem, in the moment of this particular crisis, to be having second thoughts about Matthau's games. What's clear early on is that this imminent nuclear holocaust could have been avoided by a political society that knew, and agreed, that nuclear weapons were a zero-sum game. These world powers are overconfident; even more, they're driven by ideological suspicions that exacerbate the difficulties of establishing any sense of diplomacy or trust.

It's to the point that the president, the reliable and not-easily ruffled Fonda, finds himself on the phone with the Soviet chairman practically pleading for some sense of mutual trust and allegiance between their warring countries. We never see the chairman. His sentiments are reported to us through Buck, an interpreter played by Larry Hanson whose job—contra the attitude of the know-it-alls prone to abstraction—is to try to understand the chairman as a person. This is Fonda's request: Don't only translate his words, translate the man's feelings. Treat him, in other words, like a man capable of feeling—not like an unbending war machine.

Overconfidence in technology, overconfidence in our own exceptionalism: these are the ills *Fail Safe*, an imperfect but appealing and urgent movie, diagnoses of the powers that be. That's a little different than the *other* cold war classic of 1964, Stanley Kubrick's *Dr. Strangelove; or, How I Learned to Stop Worrying and Love the Bomb*, which—likewise released by Columbia Pictures—is indelibly tied to *Fail Safe* much for that reason. The films were famously involved in a copyright infringement lawsuit on behalf of Kubrick and Peter George, whose novel *Red Alert* was the basis for *Strangelove*. To George, the similarities between his project and *Fail Safe* couldn't have been clearer. And, with Kubrick, he got his way; *Fail Safe*'s release was delayed six months, to October of that year, by which point *Strangelove* had ostensibly already rendered it moot.

The important footnote here isn't the lawsuit itself, but the coincidence in which it resulted. October 1964 put *Fail Safe* squarely in election season; the COVID crisis is also coming during an election year. In '64, the choice was between Barry Goldwater—painted, by his opponent, to be a war hawk, and very much on the wrong side of nuclear history as far as *both Fail Safe* and *Strangelove* are concerned—and Lyndon B. Johnson. We, too, are at a dire crossroads in a pivotal election—more so than even last time. Though underseen in its moment, *Fail Safe* is inextricable from Johnson's win; in its tragedy, which complements *Strangelove*'s folly, it made a better case for his election than perhaps the candidate himself did.

Since rewatching the movie, I've been hung up on that odd confluence of world politics playing out in the movies and in real life simultaneously—wondering, in part, if we'll have an era of post-COVID art to match and make sense of our current disaster, and the politics of this disaster, in the way that legions of films and books were being made and released to the public as the crises of the Cold War were happening, actively playing a role in the public discourse. The discourse of 2020 is much more diffuse. In the first place, most attempts to crack the Trump era on its own terms, COVID notwithstanding, are already failures in one way or another.

In some ways, next to *Strangelove*, *Fail Safe* is a failure as well—though really only because *Strangelove* still feels so cutting for its time, less fixated on suspense and its character's wavering moral positions than on the outright mania of this being a "situation" to begin with. *Strangelove* is the finer, more daring film. But that doesn't automatically make it a better hang—particularly in context. What I tend to crave after I watch Kubrick's manic boil of a masterpiece is an adult in the (war) room. Somebody—anybody!

Fail Safe gave me that. But it also feels more outlandish for this very reason. No, there's no cowboy riding a bomb to his own giddy destruction in Lumet's film. There's no "Bucky," the Kubrick character cartoonishly brought to life by the great George C. Scott. Instead, Lumet gives us the staid, professional Buck.

But it also provides us the fantasy of a government actively motivated to put its people first, despite certain voices in the room. Then comes the slaughter: the sacrifice. *Strangelove* may be the satire. Compared to the historical present, however, it's *Fail Safe* that reeks all the more of pure fantasy.

VANITY FAIR, MAY 8, 2020

Alamogordo, New Mexico.
Epicenter of the first atomic bomb explosion in 1945, Trinity test.
1965—Elliott Erwitt

Marilyn Monroe during the filming of *The Misfits*,
Reno, Nevada, 1960—Bruce Davidson

BLACK DESERT,
WHITE DESERT

Serge Toubiana

I N HIS AUTOBIOGRAPHY, *Timebends: A Life*, Arthur Miller describes the origins of *The Misfits* at some length. The theme first appeared as a short story published in the American magazine *Esquire* in October 1957. It was written after Miller had had to spend some time in Nevada in the spring of 1956 while waiting for a divorce from his first wife. Nevada law is notoriously lax, and the state will grant a divorce to anyone who has lived there for six weeks or more. Miller had rented a cabin at Pyramid Lake, tucked away about a hundred miles from Reno, the nearest city, where he would go once a week or so to do his shopping and get his laundry done. One of his neighbors was Saul Bellow, who was there for similar reasons. The Nevada desert provided Miller with the figures who were to be the heroes of his story: cowboys rather adrift in the modern world, free-spirited men who lived an outdoor life, making a living by catching wild horses they would then sell to be made into dog food. He was interested in the way they lived on the margins of society, outside the community. One day, two of the cowboys invited him to join their hunt for wild horses. With them was a younger man, who remained completely silent. Miller studied these men closely as they used lassos to catch the mustangs, then tethered them to large tires to prevent them escaping. He later described Pyramid Lake as 'a gray salty lake miles long, surrounded by a Paiute Indian reservation, a forbidding but beautiful place occasionally favored by movie companies shooting scenes of weird monsters in outer space.'[1]

While Miller was living in Nevada waiting to obtain his divorce and marry Marilyn Monroe, she was in Hollywood, making *Bus Stop* (1956) with director Joshua Logan. She was experiencing great difficulty in advancing her Hollywood career; to her despair, producers would only cast her as a sexy ingénue in lightweight comedies, denying her parts worthy of her talent.

She was under contract to Twentieth Century Fox and had to fulfill her commitments before setting up her own production company, Marilyn Monroe Productions, with her associate, photographer Milton Greene. This move was intended to free her from the studios, as Norman Rosten, Miller's friend, confirms when he describes how, after the success of *The Seven Year Itch* (1955), she tried to renegotiate the terms of her contract with Fox to give herself higher fees and, above all, a say on scripts and choice of directors: 'She had sensed her power; she was determined to test it. She was ready to enter the fray, to deal with the lawyers, press agents, promotion people: in short to deal.'[2] Marilyn cherished hopes of finding more dignified parts, despite the frequent jibes aimed at her in the American popular press. In his autobiography, Miller describes 'the then powerful movie columnists ... taking shots at Marilyn, the non-actor floozy, for the preposterous chutzpah of making demands on so great and noble a corporation as Twentieth Century Fox.' At this point, Marilyn was trying to change her way of life and be a good wife while she waited to be offered a 'wonderful film.' Her marriage to Miller in Connecticut on July 1, 1956 was expected to help her distance herself from the studios. After the wedding, the couple moved to New York, and Marilyn again took courses at The Actors Studio, where Lee Strasberg was teaching his 'Method,' based on Stanislavsky's theory of acting. There she made friends with Eli Wallach, with whom she would later appear in *The Misfits*.

One of the first projects of Marilyn Monroe Productions was *The Prince and the Showgirl*, an adaptation of Terence Rattigan's comedy, directed by and starring Laurence Olivier. Marilyn was thrilled to be playing opposite a great actor like Olivier, but their relationship on the set at Shepperton studios was strained, and the film was a disappointment. Miller, however, took advantage of this interlude to write his short story, *The Misfits*.

AN OFFERING FOR MARILYN

After making *The Prince and the Showgirl*, Marilyn Monroe and Arthur Miller returned to set up home in New York, spending weekends at a rented house by the sea on Long Island. In the summer of 1957, Marilyn, who wanted a child, found she was pregnant. But the pregnancy was ectopic, and she was rushed to hospital in New York. Her friend Sam Shaw, who had started taking photographs of her at the beginning of the 1950s when she was relatively unknown, came to visit her. At the hospital, he met Miller, whose *Esquire* story he had read. While they were taking a walk together, he suggested that Miller turn it into a screenplay: 'It would make a great movie and that's a woman's part she could kick into the stands.' Miller, who had previously seemed reluctant to work in the cinema, liked the idea and immediately got down to work. He wanted Marilyn to have a part written especially for her that would show the studio bosses she had the makings of an intelligent and sensitive actress with a gift for serious drama. *The Misfits* was his offering to her at a time when she had just suffered a terrible ordeal—she now knew she would never be able to have children—and was in open conflict with Fox over the direction her career should take. Her contract required that she complete two other films: *Some Like It Hot* (1959), the second film in which she was to be directed by Billy Wilder (and a runaway success); and immediately afterwards, *Let's Make Love* (1960), directed by George Cukor, in which she would play opposite Yves Montand.

In its first version, as a short story, three male characters of different ages dominate *The Misfits*: Guido, the pilot; Gay Langland, the hunter of wild horses; and Perce Howland, a young rodeo rider and a bit of a daredevil. Roslyn, the female character, hardly appears; she is Gay's wife, but they are separated. Miller summarizes it as follows: 'a story of three men who cannot locate a home on the earth for themselves and who, for something to do, catch wild horses to go to be butchered for dog food, and a woman, as homeless as they, but whose intact sense of life's sacredness suggests a meaning for existence. It was a story about the indifference I had been feeling not only in Nevada, but in the world now. We were being stunned at our powerlessness to control our lives, and Nevada was simply the perfection of our common loss.'

ROSLYN AND MARILYN

One of the paradoxes of *The Misfits* is that Marilyn Monroe hesitated for a long time before agreeing to play the part of Roslyn. 'She read parts of the screenplay and laughed delightedly at some of the cowboys' lines,' says Miller, 'but seemed to withhold full commitment to playing Roslyn.' She probably thought Roslyn was too similar to herself, almost her double, with the same problems, the same worries, the same difficulty in coping with life. Indeed, as Miller wrote the screenplay he was observing the woman who was now living with him, and who, although she had a new life and felt more protected, was as vulnerable as ever, ceaselessly struggling with the dark forces that prevented her personality blossoming. 'Her very pain bespoke life and the wrestling with the angel of death. She was a living rebuke to anyone who didn't care,' wrote Miller. Like Marilyn, Roslyn had a difficult childhood and a troubled relationship with her mother, compounded of intimacy and rejection, and they share the same anxieties and loneliness, the same feeling of abandonment and a childlike wonder where children or animals are concerned. But their ingenuous admiration turns into mistrust as soon as a man gets too close and falls in love with them. After her divorce, which comes right at the beginning of the film, Roslyn looks for a place in the world where she can be happy, while knowing in her heart of hearts that happiness is impossible. She meets the three cowboys and has a love affair with Gay Langland (played by Clark Gable), who is both lover and father-figure. After many ordeals, most notably the climactic scene in the middle of the desert when Roslyn begs the cowboys to release the wild horses, *The Misfits* ends on a note of hope as Roslyn responds to a question ('Would you ever want a kid with me?') that Gay asked her in an earlier scene: 'If there could be one person in the world, a child who could be brave from the beginning ... I was scared to when you asked me, but I'm not so much now.'

It was not long before the idea of submitting the script to John Huston emerged. Miller realized that this was a clinching argument in persuading Marilyn to agree to appear in the film; he was convinced that Marilyn would feel at ease with Huston. He had already told the story of *The Misfits* to an old friend, Frank Taylor, playing all the roles and even imitating the language of the Nevada cowboys. Taylor insisted on reading the script, and loved it. The two had known each other for years; Taylor (and Miller's first wife) had worked for a company called Reynal and Hitchcock, who had published Miller's early books, *Situation Normal* and the novel *Focus*. In the late 1940s, Taylor joined Twentieth Century Fox, hoping to develop film projects for them, including an adaptation of F. Scott Fitzgerald's *Tender is the Night*. Taylor, whom Miller describes as 'a gaunt, sophisticated man of great height ... an imaginative mix of aggressive entrepreneur and aficionado of literature,' eagerly agreed to produce the film for Seven Arts Productions, a subsidiary of United Artists. The idea of approaching Huston to direct the film probably came out of discussions between Miller and Taylor; Taylor was fortunate enough to know him personally.

THE SCRIPT SENT TO JOHN HUSTON

On July 14, 1958, before the screenplay was actually completed, Miller wrote to Huston, who was staying at his Irish country home, St Clerans, in Galway, offering to send him the script. He summed up his project briefly: 'The setting is the Nevada back country, concerns two cowboys, a pilot, a girl, and the last of the mustangs up in the mountains … The script is an early draft. If you are interested I'd want to sit and talk over my notions of further developments and of course would like to hear yours.'[3] Knowing that Huston had decided for the time being not to work in the United States—probably for tax reasons—Miller was careful to reassure him: 'Having seen so much of the earth, perhaps you'll know of a foreign locale equivalent if, in fact, it's impossible to work here.' Nine days later, on July 23, Huston replied: 'I was delighted to get your letter and flattered that you should have thought to write to me about your script. Do send it on to me right [now] and you shall hear from me about it immediately. It's true that for various reasons I prefer to do pictures outside of the United States for the present time, but making a good picture is much more important. There are, however, parts of Mexico that are identical to northern Nevada—even in wintertime.'

While Marilyn was filming *Some Like It Hot* with Billy Wilder, Miller worked on his script. On June 16, 1959, he sent a new draft to Huston, who was in London. 'Dear John, here is the beginning of the screenplay. I ought to say nothing about it until you had read it. One or two purely mechanical exchanges of dialogue are merely summarized, but the rest is fully written out. I hope to hear from you soon, and was sorry to learn that you were not coming to New York this week. I have become newly enamored with the whole story … but this time not so exclusively from a telescopic distance. I think they are people now and that this tale can break an audience's heart. I am going on with the revision because I have a great lust for it now.' Miller spent the whole summer polishing the screenplay, and sent Huston an almost final version in late September. Finally, on September 29, Huston was able to send him an enthusiastic telegram in New York: 'Dear Arthur, script magnificent. Regards, John.'

At this time, Huston was working on an ambitious project to make a film on the life of Freud, based on a screenplay by Jean-Paul Sartre. But he found Sartre's first draft too 'literary,' especially as it ran to several hundred pages. Miller's proposal came just at the right time—it would be several months before shooting could start on the *Freud* project, and Huston was far from sorry at the prospect of working with Marilyn Monroe again. Ten years previously, in 1949, he had put her through screen tests when he was preparing to make *We Were Strangers* for Columbia. 'She used to come to the set and watch the shooting … There was some talk of Columbia giving her a screen test. She was a very pretty girl, young and appealing, but so are thousands of girls in Hollywood. Such talk often leads to the casting couch rather than to the studio floor, and I suspected someone was setting her up. Something about Marilyn elicited my protectiveness, so, to forestall any hanky-panky, I expressed my readiness to do a test, in color, with John Garfield playing opposite her.'[4] The following year, when he was about to make *The Asphalt Jungle* and was looking for an actress to play Angela, the pretty mistress of the shady lawyer played by Louis Calhern, he remembered her. This screen test was a success. 'The scene she was to read called for Angela to be stretched out on a divan; there was no divan in my office, so Marilyn said, "I'd like to do the scene on the floor"... And that's the way she did it. She kicked off her shoes, lay down on the floor and read for us. When she finished, Arthur [Hornblow, the producer of the film] and I looked at each other and nodded. She was Angela to a "t".' Meanwhile, between her debut in *The Asphalt Jungle* and the shooting of *The Misfits*, Marilyn had become one of Hollywood's biggest stars. Huston, also under contract to Fox, had the reputation of being a maverick and an adventurer, a great gambler who alternated between commercial successes and disasters, a good director of actors with the useful attribute of being able to adapt to any situation.

A STAR-STUDDED FILM ON THE MARGINS OF THE HOLLYWOOD SYSTEM

Lew Wasserman, the powerful head of the MCA agency to which Marilyn Monroe and Arthur Miller were both under contract, put his whole weight behind the project. Thanks to him, Miller and Taylor were able to assemble a dream cast that fitted perfectly the choices they had originally made. At one time, they had considered Robert Mitchum for the part of Gay Langland.

Elliott Hyman, head of Seven Arts, contacted him, and he seemed interested in reading the screenplay, but did not get in touch again. On November 13, 1959, Clark Gable met Miller, who talked to him about the project, and especially about the character of Langland. Gable was very puzzled at first and wondered just what kind of a script it was: a western, or something else? Miller found a definition that settled the question: 'It's a sort of Eastern western.' After that, Gable felt ready to take the plunge.

With Montgomery Clift, on the other hand, whom they had in mind for the part of Perce, the problem was that no insurance company would cover him after the terrible car accident that had disfigured his face and intensified his self-destructive impulses. But Miller and Huston insisted on having him, and they eventually won the insurers over. Both of them were very happy with the way Clift behaved throughout the shoot, as well as with his moving portrayal of Perce. He is extraordinarily powerful in two of the film's most affecting scenes: in the first, a monologue, he calls his mother from a phone box at the side of the road just before arriving in Dayton to ride in a rodeo; in the second, lying stretched out on the floor in the back room of a saloon, he confides in Roslyn, his head resting on her knees. When these scenes were shot, Clift was word-perfect; his fellow-actors and the whole crew were amazed. The parts of Isabelle, Roslyn's landlady in Reno, and the pilot were played by Thelma Ritter and Eli Wallach, two good film actors who had also acted on the New York stage.

From its origins to its production, *The Misfits* seems like an independent film, conceived in a completely different way from the traditional studio system. The impulse behind it belonged entirely to Miller, the screenwriter, an unusual state of affairs in American cinema, where the initiative always came exclusively from the producers. But the presence of Marilyn Monroe and Clark Gable was enough to guarantee finance for the film, whose initial budget was three and a half million dollars, a reasonable sum for Hollywood at that time, given also that Monroe's and Gable's fees accounted for a significant part of it.

An atypical production like *The Misfits* was possible at the beginning of the 1960s because the industry was going through a serious crisis caused by the first effects of competition from television. The studios started investing heavily in producing TV series, and many film sets were requisitioned or adapted to the needs of the new medium. It was, therefore, a good moment for experimentation on the fringes of the big studio economy. The same year, Hitchcock made *Psycho*, an experiment carried out under the same conditions as a television show,[5] with a budget of only $800,000.

The plan was that *The Misfits* would be shot almost entirely out of doors, in the places in Reno and the Nevada desert where Miller had had the idea for the story and had come across his characters. Russell Metty, one of Hollywood's most respected cameramen, was responsible for lighting it in black and white, at a time when most studio productions, specifically to counteract the growing influence of television, were shot in color and in CinemaScope. From that point of view also, the aesthetic assumptions behind *The Misfits*, close to those of documentary, went against the grain of the traditional star vehicle. Other members of the crew were chosen from among the best technical people. They included George Tomasini, Hitchcock's regular editor; 'Doc' Erickson, the production manager, who had also worked with Hitchcock; and Steve Grimes, the art director. And when big stars are involved, it always entails additional personnel. Marilyn, for example, had her coach, Paula Strasberg (the wife of Lee Strasberg), with her throughout the shoot, as well as her personal secretary, May Reis; her masseur; her regular make-up artist; her hairdresser; her lighting stand-in; a dresser and a chauffeur. In that respect, *The Misfits* was a film like any other, except for the fact that it was to be made in high summer in the desert, far away from Hollywood and in circumstances that left a great deal of room for uncertainty.

AN EXCLUSIVE CONTRACT WITH MAGNUM

The other unique aspect of the making of the film was the exclusive contract signed by Frank Taylor with the Magnum photographic agency. Lee Jones, then in charge of special projects in Magnum's New York office, got in touch with Taylor as soon as she read about the project in the press. 'We met that morning,' Jones says, 'and it soon became clear that my idea that Magnum hold exclusive for all stills on *The Misfits* fit neatly Taylor's plans for the film. He wanted it to be elite and special from the outset.'[6] It would not be the first time that Magnum photographers had covered the making of a film, but it was the first time they had obtained exclusive rights, and with actors as famous as Monroe, Gable and Clift. Lee Jones recalls: 'Magnum had worked on other films as still photographers and each time there was a painful struggle between the publicity department's needs and expectations and Magnum's basic belief that copyright belongs to the photographer. There were predictable clashes: the producers knew that a Magnum coverage had a better chance in the major magazines and Magnum felt obligated to sell first rights to whatever publication we felt would do the photographer—and the film—the greatest good. But the publicity departments were accustomed to receiving all of the work of a commercial set photographer, and to making their own choices.' The fact that Magnum won an exclusive contract owes much to Frank Taylor's personality; Jones describes him as 'a most unusual man, he understood and admired good photography.' John Huston liked photographers too. He had been a friend of Robert Capa, who founded Magnum with Henri Cartier-Bresson and George Rodger in 1947. After Capa's death, Huston retained his connections with some of Magnum's photographers, among them Inge Morath, who had covered several of his films, including *Moulin Rouge* and *The Unforgiven*, a routine western that Huston hated. The fact that Cornell Capa, Robert's brother, was one of the photographers sent to cover *The Misfits* was bound to bring back happy memories for him.

It was agreed that Magnum would send its best photographers in teams of two, changing every fifteen days throughout shooting. Dick Rowan, an editor in the New York office, would also stay in Reno to write the captions, once permissions had been obtained from the actors, who had contractual rights over the choice of photographs. The pictures could then be sold to newspapers and magazines all over the world. The producers wanted exclusive rights over the work of photographers who were ranked among the world's best. They could well imagine that the presence of Marilyn Monroe, Clark Gable and Montgomery Clift would arouse great interest on the part of the American and foreign press. John Huston's personality, the fact that Miller would be with Marilyn while the film was being made, even the unusual idea of filming in the middle of the desert, would all create an aura of excitement. Also, as Eve Arnold, one of the photographers who was to cover the shoot, put it, the agreement with Magnum was 'calculated to take the burden of having to relate daily to different photographers from the shoulders of the actors. It was done particularly to free Marilyn of all extraneous concern.'[7]

Inge Morath and Cartier-Bresson were the first photographers to go to Reno, where the film crew had set up and where the first scenes were to be shot. Then came Dennis Stock, Eve Arnold, Ernst Haas, Cornell Capa, Bruce Davidson, Elliott Erwitt and Erich Hartmann. 'We drove from New York,' recalls Inge Morath, 'because we wanted to discover America. Each photographer did as he or she liked, with no restrictions. Marilyn was obviously the main attraction, and many of our photos were used in the press at that time.'[8] She remembers the fifteen days she spent on the set as a unique time: 'It was definitely the most fascinating film I've ever worked on, a very intense experience. You could easily see Marilyn was causing problems; she was always late, which was no fun for the others, and the film was falling behind schedule. But when she arrived, everyone was so pleased to see her!'

Cartier-Bresson, who only worked on this one film-shoot, recorded his impressions in a taped interview. In it he describes his strange meeting with Marilyn when he arrived at the shoot. He had never met her before, and was sitting in the cafeteria one evening, next to an empty place. It was reserved for Marilyn, who was late. She arrived, and was introduced to Cartier-Bresson, who had put his Leica on the seat next to his own. Marilyn hesitated for a moment, waiting for him to move it. Then Cartier-Bresson had the audacity to ask her to bless the camera. The story goes that Marilyn did this with good grace, lightly brushing the Leica as she made to sit down. 'I saw her bodily—Marilyn—for the first time,' he confided, 'and I was struck as by an apparition in a fairytale. Well, she's beautiful—anyone can notice this, and she represents a certain myth of what we call in France "la femme éternelle." On the other hand, there's something extremely alert and vivid in her, an intelligence. It's her personality, it's a glance, it's something very tenuous, very vivid, that disappears quickly, that appears again.' Inge Morath also emphasizes Marilyn's photogenic quality: 'Once she was ready [to be photographed], she would surpass the expectations of the lens. She had a shimmering quality like an emanation of water, and she moved lyrically.' Elliott Erwitt, who had covered the making of Billy Wilder's *The Seven Year Itch* and had photographed the famous scene where her white dress billows up in the draught from a subway ventilation grille, says, 'She loved photographers and the camera was crazy about her. Personally, I don't think she was especially beautiful, but in the end it didn't matter what she really looked like. It was hard to take a bad photo of her.'[9]

Along with Sam Shaw, Eve Arnold was without a doubt the photographer who had the most privileged relationship with Marilyn. She records that 'at photo sessions, she was in total control, she manipulated everything—me, the camera … She knew a lot about cameras and I had never met anyone who could make them respond the way she did. So she got what she wanted, because she wasn't under all the kinds of pressure she felt during a film-shoot: remembering her lines, enduring hours of preparation … With me, she was in charge of the situation.'

When describing their impressions of a film-shoot, set photographers often repeat the same theme: the waiting, which sometimes becomes very tedious. They have to wait for the perfect moment, when everything has been rehearsed, the light is ready, and everyone, actors and technicians, is in the right place. Then they must work as discreetly as possible, almost invisibly, surrounded by the film crew. On the set of *The Misfits*, there was a lot of waiting, as usual, but this time, everyone had to wait for Marilyn, too. 'She was perpetually late,' says Elliott Erwitt, 'or else she didn't show up at all. It was total chaos. This is what gives the photographer so much freedom to work. Photographs are always more interesting when the subjects are taken off guard or not quite where they should be.' Eve Arnold goes further when she says, 'the big gossip was always, Would Marilyn work that day?', adding that Marilyn, who had come back exhausted from making *Let's Make Love*, had admitted to her, 'I'm thirty-four years old. I've been dancing for six months ... I've had no rest, I'm exhausted. Where do I go from here?'

Dennis Stock had special responsibility within the Magnum team for photographing Montgomery Clift. 'The choice of photographers was pretty random, made by Magnum and the producer according to the shooting schedule and who was available. I didn't know Clift before this shoot, but I was known to have taken a lot of pictures of James Dean and Marlon Brando. That reputation gave me a sort of link with certain actors of that sort, people who weren't from the big cities but more often from the mid-West; James Dean came from Indiana, Brando from Kansas.'[10] Ernst Haas, on the other hand, was more interested in the rodeo scenes shot at Dayton, and in the capture of the wild horses near the salt flats, scenes involving Gable, Wallach and Clift, and their stand-ins. These difficult and dangerous scenes with the wild horses were shot in October, when filming was well under way. They required hundreds of takes, some shot from above in a plane, which Guido (Eli Wallach) was supposed to be flying so that he could drive the mustangs. The two other cowboys, Gay Langland and Perce, would then do their best to catch them with their lassos. In October, the climate in the Nevada desert had changed after weeks of tremendous heat. Now the wind, cold and dust interfered considerably with the work of the crew.

Erich Hartmann was the last photographer to cover the shoot, ten days of which had to take place at the Paramount studios in Los Angeles, starting on October 24. Huston shot several scenes there, using a back-projection method that allowed him to use his actors and give the illusion of movement by projecting images of the desert onto a screen. Hartmann's pictures reveal a rather somber mood, and the actors show signs of fatigue. It is clear that the crew will be relieved when the shoot is over.

A CHAOTIC SHOOT

The Misfits should have begun shooting on March 3, 1960, but Hollywood actors had been on a fairly solid strike; this had held up work on *Let's Make Love*, and Marilyn was not available until early July. On July 18, Huston shot his first scenes in Reno, 'The Biggest Little City in the World,' as a banner hanging over Main Street put it. During the first two days he shot only some footage of the city (which he later decided to discard), to use in the title sequence, while he waited for all the actors to arrive. In one of Inge Morath's photographs, the clapperboard shows the date, while in the background, Miller and Huston seem to be location-spotting in a Reno street, scouting like two soldiers on a recce. Cartier-Bresson has captured the rapport between the director and his scriptwriter, who were clearly delighted at getting to know each other by working on the same project. One of his photographs shows Huston doing a little dance in the middle of the street, surrounded by a crowd of onlookers who are in fact extras. Some of the photographs taken by Elliott Erwitt reveal the same playful intimacy: we see the two men deep in discussion, sitting together on a set. At that stage, *The Misfits* still seemed a promising venture.

Most of the crew were staying at Mapes Hotel, which also housed a casino where Huston would go straight away to indulge his habit. The hotel provided an entire support system for the film, with several rooms or suites turned into offices or editing suites. George Tomasini and Stewart Linder in fact began editing the film at the beginning of August, and gave Huston several rough-cuts as it was being shot. Every morning, before going to the set, Huston and his coworkers would watch the rushes at the Crest Theater, two blocks from the hotel.

Clark Gable arrived from Hollywood in his silver Mercedes coupé, a magnificent vehicle with gull-wing doors, in which he had promised himself he would break speed records on his way to the set every morning. Marilyn herself arrived from Los Angeles on July 20 and was met as she got off the plane by two hundred people, including Miller, Huston and Frank Taylor, as well as representatives of the local press. She traveled from the airport to her hotel in Taylor's convertible, and the whole town turned out to watch the parade and cheer. On July 21, Montgomery Clift checked into Mapes Hotel, before going to Pocatello, Idaho, for a few days, to learn how to handle wild horses. While he was there, he attended a rodeo, and as he was trying to help one of the wranglers mount a bull, he was knocked over and injured his nose. It seemed as if before he even started shooting, which he was supposed to do on August 12, he had got into role as Perce, the youngest of the three cowboys. In the film, Perce wears a white bandage round his head because of a rodeo injury.

The day after she arrived, Marilyn shot her first scene, the one in which she appears at the window of the house belonging to her landlady, Isabelle (Thelma Ritter), before going to the courthouse for her divorce hearing. When shooting started, the mood seemed idyllic. On July 24, Frank Taylor and his wife Nan gave a party at the house they had rented near Reno, attended by all the actors, as well as by Inge Morath and Henri Cartier-Bresson. All this scrupulously detailed information appears in a diary written by James Goode, a journalist present throughout the shoot. When the film was released, Goode published a book, *The Making of The Misfits*,[11] authorized by the producers. Reading his diary, we are able to follow the shoot day by day, to note the problems, conflicts and delays and get an objective and disinterested vision of the actual process of making the film.

But it was not long before the situation on the set became intolerable, and not only on account of the sweltering Nevada heat, or the habit Marilyn had developed of arriving late on the set every day. Never free from self-doubt, and taking one kind of medication after another, she took refuge behind Paula Strasberg, who had a very strong hold over her. Strasberg was under contract to the production as Marilyn's 'coach,' but in fact she played the role of intermediary between the actress and the rest of the crew. She was a kind of authoritarian guru, with the presumption to tell Huston the 'real' way he should direct Marilyn. 'She protected her like a mother hen, and dealt with all kinds of things for her,' reports Dennis Stock. This was calculated to irritate Huston and, even more, Miller. In the photographs of the shoot, Paula is always dressed in black, wearing dark glasses and a hat to protect her from the sun. In his autobiography, Miller is quite hard on the woman whom the crew 'promptly named ... Black Bart, or just Bart. Between takes, she would retire with Marilyn to her trailer, where when I entered, they would usually fall silent, just as they would before Huston.' When shooting moved to Pyramid Lake, where the temperature was verging on 120 degrees Fahrenheit, Strasberg is said to have sat in her air-conditioned Cadillac, making Marilyn rehearse her dialogue. To counteract what he saw as Strasberg's harmful influence, Huston used irony, 'listening to everything she had to tell him with a seriousness so profound as to be ludicrous.'

Knowing how difficult it was for Marilyn to get to the set on time every day, Huston delayed the start of shooting by an hour, but to no avail. Marilyn continued to arrive late, or not at all. Filming was suspended between August 27 and September 6 while she was in a Los Angeles clinic, suffering from exhaustion. But Huston still thought of her as a professional actress, faced with the challenge of playing a role worthy of her. 'She was taking pills to go to sleep and pills to wake up in the morning ... She seemed to be in a daze half the time. When she was herself, though, she could be marvelously effective. She wasn't acting—I mean she was not pretending to an emotion. It was the real thing,' Huston would later write in his autobiography.

More than anyone else, Miller hoped that by playing Roslyn, a role with 'the womanly dignity that part of her longed for,' Marilyn would recover self-confidence. When filming began, almost four years had elapsed since he had created the character: a child-woman whose tragic gaze overwhelms anyone who comes near her and tries to capture her soul, but who never ceases to search the heavens for the lucky star that will bring her joy. 'I hoped that by living through this role she too might arrive at some threshold of faith and confidence, even as I had to wonder if I could hold on to it myself after we had both been let down from expectations such as few people allow themselves in a marriage,' he wrote. This film was to be a gift to Marilyn, something that brought them closer together. Day by day, however, it turned into a martyrdom for her, and for its begetter. In most of the photographs where we see Marilyn at Miller's side, we sense a certain indifference, even a coldness, a lack of understanding on both sides. Miller often looks as if he is present on the set as a distant observer of the crew's work. Erich Hartmann captured the writer towards the end of filming, worn out, abstracted, absorbed in his own thoughts, his own solitude. Almost miraculously, Inge Morath managed to photograph Marilyn and Miller in their Reno hotel bedroom. It is a magnificent photograph: Marilyn is looking away, out of the window, and Miller keeps a certain distance. Everyone wanted pictures of Marilyn and Miller together,' Morath states. 'She didn't pose with Arthur, and refused to stand beside him. So I took this photo by instinct, without thinking about their relationship.'

In many of the pictures, Marilyn is alone, her face sad, concentrating on her character or learning her lines. But she achieves a sort of gaiety (probably for the photographer's benefit, and to play a kind of game with him or her) as soon as she's with Clark Gable, Eli Wallach or Montgomery Clift, co-stars with whom she was on friendly terms, even at the worst moments. When she felt involved in the scene she had to play, her face could suddenly light up and become radiant. Whether she's happy or sad, alone or in company, anxious or cheerful, wearing a genuine mask of pain or dancing as she delights in her own physicality, Marilyn's duality is what comes across most strikingly in these photographs.

In his biography of Marilyn, Donald Spoto very clearly takes her side. He confirms that because she had trouble sleeping due to stomach problems, she took tablets every night. He describes the making of the film as a kind of battle between Marilyn and the Miller–Huston duo. He is very negative about the screenplay, which, according to him, 'was full of grand but disconnected rhetoric about rugged individualism, the contemporary lack of intimacy and communication, the decline of the West and the nature of the American conscience.'[12] In his opinion, the script's main defect is that 'very little happens.' Spoto's view of the film is very narrow: *The Misfits* has nothing to do with the classic western or with traditional genre movies. It tells the story of people who are completely 'unbalanced'—the title of the French version was *Les Désaxés*, or 'The Unbalanced'—three men and two women who form an isolated little community in the vastness of Nevada. What they have in common is a sickness, a psychological wound, a 'split' that prevents them living, and it is precisely this profound disablement that makes them so touching. They have difficulty in living in a world they cannot grasp, that no longer matches their dreams. In its own way, *The Misfits* is the story of an impossible dream, set in an America where the great myths have died. That is what Spoto refuses to see in the film. But he makes an even more radical critique when he states that

Miller was settling scores with his wife by giving her a part that in some sense became the opposite of what it had been to start with. Spoto sees Miller's conception of the character of Roslyn as full of bitterness due to the fact that his relationship with Marilyn became noticeably worse during filming. He makes much of the fact that every day Miller would rewrite the following day's dialogue, scarcely giving Marilyn time to learn her lines. This only served to increase her agitation and anxiety, and helped to make her arrive later on the set every day. According to Spoto, Miller was rewriting his script in step with every change in his marital relationship, which was deteriorating as filming proceeded. He describes this method as a kind of weapon designed to destabilize Marilyn and make her act scenes that in her own life were helping to widen the gulf between them. The problem with this view is not only that it is overly Machiavellian, but also that it relies on Miller being a deus ex machina controlling the very progress of the film. What is more likely is that Miller had to rewrite the script according to precise requests from Huston, who wanted to give the scenes greater fluidity, especially as he was directing the film chronologically, following the script.

But Spoto also blames Huston, whom he sees as a sadistic director who enjoyed putting his actors in danger. On the basis of the fact that he would sometimes insist on shooting several takes of a scene in the oppressive heat, Spoto concludes that Huston, with Miller's connivance, was trying to pay Marilyn back for her lateness. He goes so far as to accuse Huston of 'the decisive sabotage' of his own film, because he spent his nights playing craps at the Mapes Hotel casino. Eve Arnold's photographs confirm this; Huston was a passionate gambler, and far from this being a secret or a hidden vice, it was part of his reputation and his legend. He refers to it freely in his memoirs: 'There was mostly craps, blackjack and roulette. Every so often a high-roller would come in, put up his bundle, get the limit raised and try to break the house. I had a marvelous time losing my ass one night and winning it back the next.' In his autobiography, Miller describes Huston with evident fascination, 'shooting craps at a table with a glass of scotch in his hand, his bush jacket as crisply pressed as if he had put it on ten minutes before. He was behind twenty-five thousand dollars. He grinned and I grinned back. It did not seem important to him, although I knew he would find it awkward paying out that much. I went up to bed. In the morning at about seven I came down for breakfast, and he was still shooting craps, still with a glass of scotch in his hand. He had won back the twenty-five grand and was now trying to win more. His bush jacket looked as neat as it had before.'

The idea that Huston and Miller were plotting against Marilyn seems implausible. What is more likely is that as work on the film proceeded, it collapsed into chaos, and that no one, neither Huston nor Miller, was able to control events. The grueling heat, the frequent changes of location and the problems inherent in filming outdoors, the difficulties and dangers of shooting the rodeo and the capture of the horses, together with all the tensions among the crew, led to a delay of several weeks. Shooting had been scheduled to last fifty days, but was not completed until

November 4, 1960, forty days late and around half a million dollars over budget. That was not the result of a cynical stratagem on the part of a director and his scriptwriter to harm the film's leading star. It was simply the reality of a shoot brought to the brink of disaster by a series of unpredictable factors.

THE PHOTOGRAPHS AS FOOTPRINTS

The nine Magnum photographers were privileged witnesses of this venture. What is striking when one first looks at the photographs is their great variety of style, as if each photographer had been able to find a personal approach to material that was colorful in itself. They have left a record that demonstrates great freedom of vision, and none of the photographs resemble hackneyed publicity shots. On the contrary, every picture elegantly speaks of a proper detachment from the chosen subject and a genuine curiosity that is never showy or malicious. All the photographers enjoyed free access to the crew, and were able to work closely and naturally with the actors as well as with Huston, Miller and the other main players. They were part of the film's 'family,' even if this family was in the process of falling apart before their eyes. But they were not aware of this at the time, and their pictures retain that true innocence that still gives them value today. They took part in the work of filming like people whose job it was to trace the 'footprints' of an individual and collective adventure in which each person's role evolved and was gradually transformed by the hazards of the weather or by personal problems.

The Magnum photographers seem to have had no wish to 'direct' their pictures, in the sense of using the actors or other leading figures on the set as subjects from whom they could hope to extract photographic 'value added.' In fact, their pictures testify to an instinctive and spontaneous capacity to adapt to the actual realities of filming; they captured the widest possible variety of postures and attitudes using two typical patterns. The first is a photograph (or series of photographs) of the scene to be filmed or in process of being filmed that re-frames all the elements of the shot in question: see the magnificent sequences taken by Inge Morath and Dennis Stock of Roslyn dancing with Guido, those of her alone in the moonlight, dancing round the tree, or Davidson's and Erwitt's pictures of Marilyn playing paddle ball in the Dayton saloon. The second is an oblique view of a set, showing people in a variety of very diverse positions: it could be taken during time out or at rehearsal, when the actors are relaxing, concentrating hard or being made-up, or it could show various peripheral activities on the set.

The only series of photographs 'directed' by the Magnum photographers is the one in which Ernst Haas, Bruce Davidson and Elliott Erwitt try, one by one, and with visible difficulty, to get all the actors to pose together, around Miller, Huston and Frank Taylor. Taylor wanted this group photograph, no doubt for publicity purposes, even if it was just in order to preserve an 'official' image of the film: 'I was endlessly concerned about getting a group shot (Huston, Taylor, Gable, Miller, Monty Clift, Eli Wallach and Marilyn Monroe), but every time I suggested it everyone threw up their hands in horror—the thought of trying to assemble everyone seemed impossible.' In the photos taken by Ernst Haas, Huston and Gable are sitting on the rungs of ladders, while Marilyn turns her back just at that moment. The others are absent or off-camera. One or more of the main players are missing from several of the photos in the series. But when they are all finally together, Marilyn poses in an overly obvious way (this is clearly not the kind of photo she likes or to which she gives of her best), and others move or seem uninterested in the lens, so that it is still impossible to get a 'good' group photograph. However, Elliott Erwitt had developed a stratagem. Three days previously, he had arranged a simple set—two ladders, a stool, a crate and some parachute silk—in a courtyard adjoining the Dayton saloon. 'He created enormous curiosity about it,' describes Frank Taylor, 'but refused to tell anyone what it was about. He picked a day when everything seemed to be going smoothly—he asked us all to convene—it was probably a lunch break or when we were waiting for the sun to appear from behind a cloud—he just gathered us under the silk—Marilyn and Monty were intrigued and played around and joked—it was fun and spontaneous and suddenly it was done.' But if you look at it carefully, this group photograph looks artificial, even sinister; each person is posing for him- or herself, clearly alone, indifferent to the others. Erwitt himself admits, 'Personally, I don't think it's so great. It's been seen a lot and been much in demand, but it's less interesting from the photographic point of view than for the people in it. It just so happened that everyone was available at that moment.'

In the years since 1960, the Magnum photographers have become well aware that their experience in the three months when, in turns, they lived in the Nevada desert, was unique. What they did not know was that *The Misfits*, the processes of whose making they had followed closely day by day, would have such a tragic ending. In the words of Dennis Stock, 'It was one of the very last occasions when you could find that kind of intimacy between the photographers and the stars they were photographing, and this shows in the pictures. It was all like a sort of free for all, because we had nothing to lose.' As Inge Morath says, 'It also marked the end of a certain type of cinema, in which the photographers were free to move about, and take their photos using the film lighting. Today it's boring to be a photographer at a shoot; everyone wants to control their own image, everyone has their agent. A certain kind of artistic generosity has disappeared. On the set of *The Misfits*, there were still hundreds of freely available images, and that's what makes the material unique. Even Marilyn, while she did control her image, gave a lot of herself, spontaneously … and Clark Gable, who was a big star, didn't make a big thing of it, and always made himself available to us.'

All these photographs form an invaluable visual record, capturing the lighting of the film, both of actors and landscapes, and recreating the atmosphere of a shoot. Brought together here like a jigsaw puzzle, they bear witness to a unique experience, fixing forever each person's state of mind, their anxieties and enthusiasm and their moments of weariness and hope as a film was in the process of being made. They

are like fireflies, lighting up the dark skies of people looking
for their lucky star.

Shooting of *The Misfits* was completed on November 4, 1960.
The following day, Clark Gable had a heart attack and was
admitted to hospital in Hollywood. He died on November 16
after a second attack, without being able to see the final version
of the film. Montgomery Clift was already preparing to play
another demanding role, Freud, for Huston. Relations between
the two deteriorated to the point that the five-month-long shoot
of *Freud: A Secret Passion* became a torment for Clift, an actor
marked by his air of fragility and his delicate, expressive features.
As soon as *The Misfits* was finished, Marilyn made public her
separation from Miller. He returned alone to New York, while
she was about to start a new film, *Something's Got to Give*, directed
by George Cukor, which she was unable to finish. She died on
August 5, 1962, in mysterious and tragic circumstances that
have still not been fully explained. The image of Roslyn in *The
Misfits* is thus the last we have of her on the screen. No one
today can be in any doubt that it is the image of a great actress.

TRANSLATED BY IMOGEN FORSTER

Sources

1. Arthur Miller, *Timebends: A Life* (New York, 1987).
2. Sam Shaw and Norman Rosten, *Marilyn Among Friends* (London, 1987).
3. John Huston Collection, Margaret Herrick Library, Academy of Motion Pictures.
4. John Huston, *An Open Book* (New York, 1980).
5. François Truffaut, *Hitchcock* (New York, 1967).
6. As told to Clélia Cohen and the author, July 1999.
7. Eve Arnold, *Marilyn Monroe: An Appreciation* (New York, 1987).
8. Interview with the author, September 23, 1998.
9. Interview with Alain Bergala for Magnum Cinéma (Paris, 1994).
10. Interview with the author, June 25, 1999.
11. James Goode, *The Making of The Misfits* (New York, 1961).
12. Donald Spoto, *Marilyn Monroe: The Biography* (London, 1993).

"I never knew anyone who even came close to Marilyn in natural ability to use both photographer and still camera. Because we were both inexperienced and didn't know what shouldn't be done, we improvised and made things work. Over the years I have found myself in the privileged position of photographing someone who had not merely a gift for the still camera, as I had first thought, but a genius for it."—Eve Arnold, *Film Journal*

Marilyn Monroe, Nevada, 1960—Eve Arnold

1960, Eve Arnold

1960, Eve Arnold

MARILYN MONROE AND
THE LOVELESS WORLD

Jonas Mekas

M ARILYN MONROE, the saint of the Nevada Desert. When everything else has been said about *The Misfits*, how bad the film is and all that, she still remains there, MM, the saint. And she haunts you, you'll never forget her.

It is MM that is the film. A woman who has known love, has known life, has known men, has been betrayed by all three, but has retained her dream of man, love, and life.

She meets these tough men, Gable, Clift, Wallach, in her search for love and life; and she finds love everywhere and she cries for everyone. It's MM that is the only beautiful thing in the whole ugly desert, in the whole world, in this whole dump of toughness, atom bomb, death.

Everybody has given up their dreams, all the tough men of the world have become cynics, except MM. And she fights for her dream—for the beautiful, innocent, and free. It is she who fights for love in the world, when the men fight only wars and act tough. Men gave up the world. It is MM who tells the truth in this movie, who accuses, judges, reveals. And it is MM who runs into the middle of the desert and in her helplessness shouts: *"You are all dead, you are all dead!"*—in the most powerful image of the film—and one doesn't know if she is saying those words to Gable and Wallach or to the whole loveless world.

Is MM playing herself or creating a part? Did Miller and Huston create a character or simply re-create MM? Maybe she is even talking her own thoughts, her own life? Doesn't matter much. There is so much truth in her little details, in her reactions to cruelty, to false manliness, nature, life, death, that she is overpowering, one of the most tragic and contemporary characters of modern cinema, and another contribution to The Woman as a Modern Hero in Search of Love (see *Another Sky*, *The Lovers*, *Hiroshima, Mon Amour*, *The Savage Eye*, etc., etc.).

It is strange how cinema, bit by bit, can piece together a character. Cinema is not only beautiful compositions or well-knit stories; cinema is not only visual patterns or play of light. Cinema also creates human characters.

We are always looking for "art," or for good stories, drama, ideas, content in movies—as we are accustomed to in books. Why don't we forget literature and drama and Aristotle! Let's watch the face of man on the screen, the face of MM, as it changes, reacts. No drama, no ideas, but a human face in all its nakedness—something that no other art can do. Let's watch this face, its movements, its shades; it is this face, the face of MM, that is the content and the story and idea of the film, that is the whole world, in fact.

VILLAGE VOICE, FEBRUARY 9, 1961

Rosemary Williams, Show Girl, 1949—Stanley Kubrick

BEYOND THE STARS

Jeremy Bernstein

T o most people, including us, the words "science-fiction movie" bring up visions of super-monsters who have flames shooting out of at least one eye while an Adonislike Earthman carries Sylvanna, a stimulating blonde, to a nearby spaceship. It is a prospect that has often kept us at home. However, we are happy to report, for the benefit of science-fiction buffs—who have long felt that, at its best, science fiction is a splendid medium for conveying the poetry and wonder of science—that there will soon be a movie for *them*. We have this from none other than the two authors of the movie, which is to be called "Journey Beyond the Stars"—Stanley Kubrick and Arthur C. Clarke.

It is to be based on a forthcoming novel called "Journey Beyond the Stars," by Arthur C. Clarke and Stanley Kubrick. Mr. Clarke and Mr. Kubrick, who have been collaborating on the two projects for over a year, explained to us that the order of the names in the movie and the novel was reversed to stress Mr. Clarke's role as a science-fiction novelist (he has written dozens of stories, many of them regarded as modern science-fiction classics) and Mr. Kubrick's role as a movie-maker (his most recent film was *Dr. Strangelove*).

Our briefing session took place in the living room of Mr. Kubrick's apartment. When we got there, Mr. Kubrick was talking on a telephone in the next room, Mr. Clarke had not yet arrived, and three lively Kubrick daughters—the eldest is eleven—were running in and out with several young friends. We settled ourself in a large chair, and a few minutes later the doorbell rang. One of the little girls went to the door and asked, "Who is it?" A pleasantly English-accented voice answered, through the door, "It's Clarke," and the girls began jumping up and down and saying, "It's Clark Kent!"—a reference to another well-known science-fiction personality. They opened the door, and in walked Mr. Clarke, a cheerful-looking man in his forties. He was carrying several manila envelopes, which, it turned out, contained parts of "Journey Beyond the Stars." Mr. Kubrick then came into the room carrying a thick pile of diagrams and charts, and looking like the popular conception of a nuclear physicist who has been interrupted in the middle of some difficult calculations. Mr. Kubrick and Mr. Clarke sat down side by side on a sofa, and we asked them about their joint venture.

Mr. Clarke said that one of the basic problems they've had to deal with is how to describe what they are trying to do. "Science-fiction films have always meant monsters and sex, so we have tried to find another term for our film," said Mr. C.

"About the best we've been able to come up with is a space Odyssey—comparable, in some ways to the Homeric 'Odyssey,'" said Mr. K. "It occurred to us that for the Greeks the vast stretches of the sea must have had the same sort of mystery and remoteness that space has for our generation, and that the far-flung islands Homer's wonderful characters visited were no less remote to them than the planets our spacemen will soon be landing on are to us. 'Journey' also shares with the 'Odyssey' a concern for wandering, exploration, and adventure."

Mr. Clarke agreed, and went on to tell us that the new film is set in the near future, at a time when the moon will have been colonized and space travel, at least around the planetary system, will have become commonplace. "Since we will soon be visiting the planets, it naturally occurs to one to ask whether, in the past, anybody has come to Earth to visit us," he said. "In 'Journey Beyond the Stars,' the answer is definitely yes, and the Odyssey unfolds as our descendants attempt to make contact with some extraterrestrial explorers. There will be no women among those who make the trip, although there will be some on Earth, some on the moon, and some working in space."

Relieved, we asked where the film was to be made, and were told that it would be shot in the United States and several foreign countries.

"How about the scenes Out There?" we inquired.

Mr. Kubrick explained that they would be done with the aid of a vast assortment of cinematic tricks, but he added emphatically that everything possible would be done to make each scene completely authentic and to make it conform to what is known to physicists and astronomers. He and Mr. Clarke feel that while there will be dangers in space, there will also be wonder, adventure, and beauty, and that space is a source of endless knowledge, which may transform a civilization in the same way that the voyages of the Renaissance transformed the Dark Ages. They want all these elements to come through in the film. Mr. Kubrick told us that he has been a reader of science-fiction and popular-science books, including Mr. Clarke's books on space travel, for many years, and that he has become increasingly disturbed by the barrier between scientific knowledge and the general public. He has asked friends basic questions like how many stars there are in our galaxy, he went on, and has discovered that most people have no idea at all. "The answer is a hundred billion, and sometimes they stretch their imaginations and say maybe four or five million," he said.

Speaking almost simultaneously, Mr. Clarke and Mr. Kubrick said that they hoped their film would give people a real understanding of the facts and of the overwhelming implications that the facts have for the human race.

We asked when the film will be released.

Mr. Kubrick told us that they are aiming for December, 1966, and explained that the longest and hardest part of the job will be designing the "tricks," even though the ones they plan to use are well within the range of modern cinematic technology.

When we had been talking for some time, Mr. Clarke said he had to keep another appointment, and left. After he had gone, we asked Mr. Kubrick how *Dr. Strangelove* had been received abroad. It had been shown all over the world, he told us, and had received favorable criticism everywhere, except, oddly, in Germany. He was not sure why this was, but thought it might reflect the German reliance on our nuclear strength and a consequent feeling of uneasiness at any attempt to make light of it. He said that his interest in the whole question of nuclear weapons had come upon him suddenly, when it struck him that here he was, actually in the same world with the hydrogen bomb, and he didn't know how he was learning to live with that fact.

Before making *Dr. Strangelove*, he read widely in the literature dealing with atomic warfare.

We said goodbye shortly afterward, and on our way out a phrase of J.B.S. Haldane's came back to us: "The Universe is not only stranger than we imagine; it is stranger than we *can* imagine."

The New Yorker, April 24, 1965

Stanley Kubrick on the set of *2001: A Space Odyssey*

COMING: *NASHVILLE*

Pauline Kael

I S THERE SUCH A THING as an orgy for movie-lovers—but an orgy without excess? At Robert Altman's new, almost-three-hour film, *Nashville*, you don't get drunk on images, you're not overpowered—you get elated. I've never before seen a movie I loved in quite this way: I sat there smiling at the screen, in complete happiness. It's a pure emotional high, and you don't come down when the picture is over; you take it with you. In most cases, the studio heads can conjecture what a director's next picture will be like, and they feel safe that way—it's like an insurance policy. They can't with Altman, and after United Artists withdrew its backing from *Nashville*, the picture had to be produced independently, because none of the other major companies would take it on. U.A.'s decision will probably rack up as a classic boner, because this picture is going to take off into the stratosphere—though it has first got to open. (Paramount has picked up the distribution rights but hasn't yet announced an opening date.) *Nashville* is a radical, evolutionary leap.

Altman has prepared us for it. If this film had been made earlier, it might have been too strange and new, but in the five years since he broke through with *M*A*S*H* he's experimented in so many directions that now, when it all comes together for him, it's not really a shock. From the first, packed frames of a recording studio, with Haven Hamilton (Henry Gibson), in bespangled, embroidered white cowboy clothes, like a short, horseless Roy Rogers, singing, "We must be doing somethin' right to last two hundred years," the picture is unmistakably Altman—as identifiable as a paragraph by Mailer when he's really racing. *Nashville* is simply "the ultimate Altman movie" we've been waiting for. Fused, the different styles of prankishness of *M*A*S*H* and *Brewster McCloud* and *California Split* become Jovian adolescent humor. Altman has already accustomed us to actors who don't look as if they're acting; he's attuned us to the comic subtleties of a multiple-track sound system that makes the sound more live than it ever was before; and he's evolved an organic style of moviemaking that tells a story without the clanking of plot. Now he dissolves the frame, so that we feel the continuity between what's on the screen and life off-camera.

Nashville isn't organized according to patterns that you're familiar with, yet you don't question the logic. You get it from the rhythms of the scenes. The picture is at once a *Grand Hotel*-style narrative, with twenty-four linked characters; a country-and-western musical; a documentary essay on Nashville and American life; a meditation on the love affair between performers and audiences; and an Altman party. In the opening sequences, when Altman's people—the performers we associate with him because he has used them in ways no one else would think of, and they've been filtered through his sensibility—start arriving, and pile up in a traffic jam on the way from the airport to the city, the movie suggests the circus procession at the non-ending of *8½*. But Altman's clowns are far more autonomous; they move and intermingle freely, and the whole movie is their procession. *Nashville* is, above all, a celebration of its own performers. Like Bertolucci, Altman (he includes an homage to *Last Tango in Paris*) gives the actors a chance to come out—to use more of themselves in their characters. The script is by Joan Tewkesbury, but the actors have been encouraged to work up material for their roles, and not only do they do their own singing but most of them wrote their own songs—and wrote them in character. The songs distill the singers' lives, as the mimes and theatrical performances did for the actors in *Children of Paradise*. The impulse behind all Altman's innovations has been to work on more levels than the conventional film does, and now—despite the temporary sound mix and the not-quite-final edit of the print he ran recently, informally, for a few dozen people in New York, before even the Paramount executives had seen the picture—it's apparent that he needed the technical innovations in order to achieve this union of ideas and feelings. *Nashville* coalesces lightly and easily, as if it had just been tossed off. We float while watching, because Altman never lets us see the sweat. Altman's art, like Fred Astaire's, is the great American art of making the impossible look easy.

Altman does for Nashville what he was trying to do for Houston in *Brewster McCloud*, but he wasn't ready to fly then, and the script didn't have enough layers—he needs ideas that mutate, and characters who turn corners. Joan Tewkesbury has provided him with a great subject. Could there be a city with wilder metaphoric overtones than Nashville, the Hollywood of the C. & W. recording industry, the center of fundamentalist music and pop success? The country sound is a twang with longing in it; the ballads are about poor people with no hope. It's the simplistic music of the conquered South; the songs tell you that although you've failed and you've lived a terrible, degrading life, there's a place to come home to, and that's where you belong. Even the saddest song is meant to be reassuring to its audience: the insights never go beyond common poverty, job troubles, and heartaches, and the music never rises to a level that would require the audience to reinterpret its experience. Country stars are symbolic ordinary figures. In this, they're more like political demagogues than artists. The singer bears the burden of what he has become, and he keeps saying, "I may be driving an expensive car, but that doesn't mean I'm happier than you are." Neither he nor the politician dares to come right out and confess to the audience that what he's got is what he set out for from the beginning. Instead, he says, "It's only an accident that puts me here and you there—don't we talk the same language?" Listening to him, people can easily feel that he owes them, and everybody who can sing a little or who has written a tune tries to move in close to the performers as a way of getting up there into the fame business.

Nashville is about the insanity of a fundamentalist culture in which practically the whole population has been turned into groupies. The story spans the five days during which a political manager, played by Michael Murphy, lines up the talent for a Nashville rally to be used as a TV show promoting the Presidential candidacy of Hal Phillip Walker. Walker's slogan is "New Roots for the Nation"—a great slogan for the South, since country music is about a longing for roots that don't exist.

Because country singing isn't complex, either musically or lyrically, Altman has been able to create a whole constellation of country stars out of actors. Some of them had actually cut records, but they're not primarily country singers, and their songs are never just numbers. The songs are the story being told, and even the way the singers stand—fluffing out a prom-queen dress, like Karen Black, or coolly staring down the audience, like the almond-eyed, slightly withdrawn Cristina Raines—is part of it. During this movie, we begin to realize that all that the people are is what we see. Nothing is held back from us, nothing is hidden.

When Altman—who is the most atmospheric of directors—discusses what his movies are about, he makes them sound stupid, and he's immediately attacked in the press by people who take his statements literally. (If pinned to the wall by publicity men, how would Joyce have explained the "Nighttown" sequence of *Ulysses*?) The complex outline of *Nashville* gives him the space he needs to work in, and he tells the story by suggestions, echoes, recurrences. It may be he's making a joke about how literally his explanations have been taken when in this picture the phony sentiments that turn up in the lyrics recur in other forms, where they ring true. Haven Hamilton, the bantam king of Nashville, with a red toupee for a crown, sings a maudlin piece of doggerel, with a heavy, churchy beat, about a married man's breaking up with his girlfriend ("For the sake of the children, we must say goodbye"). Later, it's almost a reprise when we see Lily Tomlin, as the gospel-singing wife of Haven's lawyer, Ned Beatty, leave Keith Carradine (the hot young singer in a trio) for exactly that reason. Throughout, there are valid observations made to seem fake by a slimy inflection. Geraldine Chaplin, as Opal, from the BBC, is doing a documentary on Nashville; she talks in flights of poetic gush, but nothing she says is as fatuous as she makes it sound. What's funny about Opal is that her affectations are all wasted, since the hillbillies she's trying to impress don't know what she's talking about. Opal is always on the fringe of the action; her opposite is the figure that the plot threads converge on—Barbara Jean (Ronee Blakley), whose ballads are her only means of expressing her yearnings. Barbara Jean is the one tragic character: her art comes from her belief in imaginary roots.

The movies often try to do portraits of artists, but their artistry must be asserted for them. When we see an actor playing a painter and then see the paintings, we don't feel the relation. And even when the portrait is of a performing artist, the story is almost always of how the artist achieves recognition rather than of what it is that has made him an artist. Here, with Ronee Blakley's Barbara Jean, we perceive what goes into the art, and we experience what the unbalance of life and art can do to a person. When she was a child, Barbara Jean memorized the words on a record and earned fifty cents in a contest, and she's been singing ever since; the artist has developed, but the woman hasn't. She has driven herself to the point of having no identity except as a performer. She's in and out of hospitals, and her manager husband (Allen Garfield) treats her as a child, yet she's a true folk artist; the Nashville audience knows she's the real thing and responds to the purity of her gift. She expresses the loneliness that is the central emotion in country music. But she isn't *using* the emotion, as the other singers do: it pours right out of her—softly. Arriving at the airport, coming home after a stretch of treatment—for burns, we're told—she's radiant, yet so breakable that it's hard to believe she has the strength to perform. A few days later, when she stands on the stage of the Opry Belle and sings "Dues," with the words "It hurts so bad, it gets me down," her fragility is so touching and her swaying movements are so seductively musical that, perhaps for the first time on the screen, one gets the sense of an artist's being consumed by her gift. This is Ronee Blakley's first movie, and she puts most movie hysteria to shame; she achieves her effects so simply that I wasn't surprised when someone near me started to cry during one of her songs. She has a long sequence on the stage of the Opry Belle when Barbara Jean's mind starts to wander and, instead of singing, she tells out-of-place, goofy stories about her childhood. They're the same sort of stories that have gone into her songs, but without the transformation they're just tatters that she clings to—and they're all she's got. Ronee Blakley, who wrote this scene, as well as the music and lyrics of all her songs, is a peachy, dimpled brunette, in the manner of the movie stars of an earlier era; as Barbara Jean, she's like the prettiest girl in high school, the one the people in town say is just perfect-looking, like Linda Darnell. But she's more delicate; she's willowy and regal, tipping to one side like the Japanese ladies carved in ivory. At one point, she sings with the mike in one hand, the other hand tracing the movements of the music in the air, and it's an absolutely ecstatic moment.

Nashville isn't in its final shape yet, and all I can hope to do is suggest something of its achievement. Altman could make a film of this magnitude for under two million dollars because he works with actors whose range he understands. He sets them free to give their own pulse to their characters; inspired themselves, they inspire him. And so we get motifs that bounce off each other—tough-broad Barbara Baxley's drunken fix on the murdered Kennedys, Shelley Duvall's total absorption in celebrity, a high-school band of majorettes twirling rifles, and Robert Doqui's anger at a black singer for not being black enough. All the allusions tell the story of the great American popularity contest. Godard was trying to achieve a synthesis of documentary and fiction and personal essay in the early sixties, but Godard's Calvinist temperament was too cerebral. Altman, from a Catholic background, has what Joyce had: a love of the supreme juices of everyday life. He can put unhappy characters on the screen (Keenan Wynn plays a man who loses the wife he's devoted to) and you don't wish you didn't have to watch them; you accept their unhappiness as a piece of the day, as you do in *Ulysses*. You don't recoil from the moody narcissism of Keith Carradine's character: there he is in his bedroom, listening to his own tapes, with one bed partner after another—with Geraldine Chaplin, whom he'll barely remember the next day, and with Lily Tomlin, whom he'll remember forever. You don't recoil, as you do in movies like *Blow-Up* or *Petulia*, because Altman wants you to be part of the life he shows you and to feel the exhilaration of being alive. When you get caught up in his way of seeing, you no longer anticipate what's coming, because Altman doesn't deliver what years of moviegoing have led you to expect. You get something else. Even when you feel in your bones what has to happen—as you do toward the climax of *Nashville*, when the characters assemble for the rally at the Parthenon and Barbara Jean, on the stage, smiles ravishingly at her public—he delivers it in a way you didn't expect. Who watching the pious Haven Hamilton sing the evangelical "Keep A'Goin'," his eyes flashing with a paranoid gleam as he keeps the audience under surveillance, would guess that the song represented his true spirit, and that when injured he would think of the audience before himself? Who would expect that Barbara Harris, playing a runaway wife—a bombed-out groupie hovering around the action—would finally get her chance onstage, and that her sexy, sweetly shell-shocked look would, at last, fit in perfectly? For the viewer, *Nashville* is a constant discovery of overlapping connections. The picture says, This is what America is, and I'm part of it. *Nashville* arrives at a time when America is congratulating itself for having got rid of the bad guys who were pulling the wool over people's eyes. The movie says that it isn't only the politicians who live the big lie—the big lie is something we're all capable of trying for. The candidate, Hal Phillip Walker, never appears on the screen; he doesn't need to—the screen is full of candidates. The name of Walker's party doesn't have to stand for anything: that's why it's the Replacement Party.

Nashville isn't full of resolutions, because Altman doesn't set up conflicts; the conflicts, as in Lily Tomlin's character, are barely visible. Her deepest tensions play out in the quietest scenes in the movie; she's a counterbalance to the people squabbling about whatever comes into their heads. There's no single reason why anybody does anything in this movie, and most of the characters' concerns are mundane. Altman uses a *Grand Hotel* mingling of characters without giving false importance to their unions and collisions, and the rally itself is barely pivotal. A lot happens in the five days, but a lot happens in any five days. There are no real dénouements, but there are no loose ends, either: Altman doesn't need to wrap it all up, because the people here are too busy being alive to be locked in place. Frauds who are halfway honest, they're true to their own characters. Even the stupidest among them, the luscious bimbo Sueleen (Gwen Welles), a tone-deaf waitress in the airport coffee shop, who wiggles and teases as she sings to the customers, and even the most ridiculous—Geraldine Chaplin's Opal—are so completely what they are that they're irresistible. At an outdoor party at Haven Hamilton's log-cabin retreat, the chattering Opal remarks, "Pure, unadulterated Bergman," but then, looking around, she adds, "Of course, the people are all wrong for Bergman, aren't they?" *Nashville* is the funniest epic vision of America ever to reach the screen.

The New Yorker, MARCH 3, 1975

COMING AROUND
THE MOUNTAIN:
CLOSE ENCOUNTERS OF
THE THIRD KIND

Matt Zoller Seitz

A S A CHILD GROWING UP in suburban Phoenix, Arizona, during the 1950s, Steven Spielberg was fascinated by the concept of UFOs and life on other worlds. His youthful obsession bore spectacular fruit: decades later, this movie-and-TV-crazy suburban boy grew up to become an expressive director whose first three features—the made-for-television movie *Duel* (1971), *The Sugarland Express* (1974) and *Jaws* (1975)—coupled precision-tooled suspense narratives with an uncanny understanding of how middle-class Americans thought, felt, and dreamed. His nautical horror film, *Jaws*, released in the summer of 1975, became the top grossing film of the 1970s. It was succeeded two years later by the space fantasy *Star Wars* (1977), directed by his old friend and future co-producer, George Lucas, who would later partner with him on the *Indiana Jones* series.

Spielberg's own 1977 release, *Close Encounters of the Third Kind*, about the effects of extraterrestrial contact on a handful of middle-class Indiana suburbanites, didn't unseat Lucas's high-tech cliffhanger in the box office record books, but it was arguably the decade's most complex, moving, and mysterious blockbuster; a spectacle that deployed the latest in miniature, optical, and sound effects to suggest not just what extraterrestrial life might look like, but how proof of its existence might make us feel. The film's unofficial sequel *E.T.* (1982), a rapturously intense kids movie about the friendship between a fatherless suburban boy and a stranded alien botanist, did topple *Star Wars* from its box-office perch, establishing Spielberg not just as the most technically fluent and financially successful director of the modern age, but also the most emotionally intuitive.

Close Encounters begins with a black screen backed by ominously shapeless chords composed by longtime Spielberg collaborator John Williams; the music rises in pitch, climaxing with a burst of music and blinding white light. Thus does the director summarize, in a few brilliant seconds, the keys to his artistic strategy: the opposing poles of mystery and certainty, darkness and illumination, fear and reassurance. Audaciously invoking fairy tales and miracles (including clips from the 1956 version of *The Ten Commandments* and a Warner Bros. cartoon with Marvin the Martian—an unwitting harbinger of his 2005 *War of the Worlds* remake—plus overheard snippets of "When You Wish Upon a Star" from Disney's 1940 film *Pinocchio*), Spielberg dares to take extraterrestrial visitation seriously as both a relatable human experience and fodder for a serious work of popular art, portraying its life-altering effect on the lives of everyday Americans.

In the first act, the film's hero, Roy Neary (Richard Dreyfuss), a suburban electrician and family man, crisscrosses the Indiana countryside in his battered pickup, attempting to restore order (light) to a state plunged into chaos (darkness) by UFO visitations. At a crossroads, his truck is nuked by light so intense that it sunburns half his face. Tracking the saucers via radio reports, Roy crosses paths with a suburban single mom, Jillian (Melinda Dillon), who's chasing her five-year-old son, Barry (Cary Guffey), a wide-eyed moppet lured from his spacious woodland home by unseen visitors. Roy, Jillian, and Barry witness a flyby visitation from starships that roll through the air like Christmas tree ornaments. Imprinted by the aliens with visions of a flat-topped mountain, these ordinary folks become hopeless seekers, grasping after a truth that's more emotional than scientific.

Although Spielberg is frequently accused of sugarcoating the fantastic, the second act of *Close Encounters* depicts these same everyday visionaries as the secular equivalent of religious pilgrims whose glimpse of infinity wrecks their lives. Paul Schrader, who did uncredited work on the film's early script, envisioned the heroes' encounter with a higher life-form as a biblical event akin to Paul's revelation on the road to Damascus. Jillian's son is kidnapped by the visitors for an unknown purpose (seeing the lights tumbling down from lightning-spackled storm clouds, the grinning kid cries, "Toys!"), then she spends the rest of the film attempting to reunite with him. Roy tries to materially recreate his subconscious visit, spiraling into derangement, building mountains from mashed potatoes, ripping up the family garden to acquire vegetation and dirt for his sculpture of what he'll later understand to be the aliens' landing place, and driving away his wife and kids. (The visitation turns workaday

Americans into artists: Jillian draws sketches of her dream, while Roy makes sculptures.)

A newscast about a chemical spill at Devil's Tower, Wyoming, puts longitude and latitude to Roy and Jillian's dream of the heavens descending upon a mountaintop: they make their way West (the classic American journey) but are captured by the military, which concocted the chemical-spill story to keep civilians from intruding on the government's first meeting with the aliens. (The chief UFO researcher, Lacombe, is played by the French New Wave figurehead François Truffaut, a movie critic turned filmmaker whom Spielberg considered a hero; by casting Truffaut, the young director instantly gave a populist sci-fi movie the art-house equivalent of street cred—and implied that even expensive Hollywood blockbusters could be personal.)

Undaunted, the duo escapes government custody, makes their way to the other side of the mountain to a state-constructed landing strip, and are rewarded with a biblically fantastic sound-and-light show in which a sky full of UFOs serves as a mere curtain-raiser. After a period of ominous silence, the mothership rises up from behind Devil's Tower like a demon disgorged from the earth, the rumbling of its engines rattling theaters' then new Dolby surround-sound systems. Spielberg's concise, abstract opening is elaborated upon in the film's finale, which sees the mothership darkening all who gaze up at its majesty, then illuminating every corner of the screen with music and light before releasing several decades' worth of abductees, including Barry. The man-child Roy, divested of everything but his desire to leave this earth, is tapped as the aliens' only human passenger on the return home—faith and innocence rewarded. Throughout the finale, Spielberg cloaks the aliens in ethereal light and presents them in suggestive flashes. Like characters in a dream, their motives and actions are never explained—yet the director's beatific images and increasingly sweet music tell us they mean no harm and that humanity is elevated by their presence.

With a brio that would become one of his signatures, the director plunges his audiences into darkness, then blinds them with light, yet for most viewers, the strategy feels liberating rather than bullying; the sure-handed tricks of a master showman. Directors love to play God, but only Spielberg makes a career of it, and makes the act seem not blasphemous or cynical, but playful and divine.

The movie seems in retrospect the most revealing early work by a private, somewhat cagey director who has largely eschewed straight-ahead memoir-type projects throughout his career, while offering glimpses of his interior that are coded by genre tropes and sometimes by historical frameworks: *Saving Private Ryan* (1998) was undertaken partly as a means of understanding his Second World War veteran father; *E.T.*, *Empire of the Sun* (1987) and *Catch Me If You Can* (2002) expressed his childhood feelings of alienation and loneliness, the pain of his parents' separation, and his own willed self-sufficiency in the aftermath; *Schindler's List* (1993), *Munich* (2005) and *The Fabelmans* (2022) are his direct reckonings with his cultural and spiritual heritage as a Jewish American filmmaker. The genocidal nightmare imagery of the *Indiana Jones* films and *War of the Worlds* feels like the director entering that part of his psyche through a side door, as does *A.I.* (2001), a posthumous collaboration with Stanley Kubrick, about a robot boy abandoned by his human mother, that includes a "Flesh Fair" sequence that's equal parts slave auction, concentration camp torture facility, redneck monster truck rally, and mass lynching.

Close Encounters is a fantasy, but its grounding in the gritty details of everyday American life makes it a much more direct expression of the longings, fears, and drives that motivated Spielberg as an artist and a man. This was illustrated most strongly in Spielberg's only directly autobiographical (though fictionalized) film, *The Fabelmans,* co-written with his *Munich, Lincoln* (2012), and *West Side Story* (2021) collaborator, Tony Kushner. It focuses on the divorce of his parents (played by Michelle Williams and Paul Dano) and the young Spielberg avatar's contemporaneous drive to master filmmaking and use storytelling to exorcize his demons and express himself as an artist. Spielberg disavowed the ending of *Close Encounters* a couple of decades after its first release, stating that if he'd made it later, he never would have presented a parent abandoning his family as a happy ending, but that's precisely what the mother character in *The Fabelmans* does, with the eventual (though pained) blessing of the family she leaves behind. In the refracted light of *The Fabelmans*, *Close Encounters* seems like Spielberg's first attempt at making the American blockbuster version of one of Truffaut's Antoine Doinel films, a series of five films that began with *The 400 Blows* (1959). Only in this one, it's not the mother who abandons her family to pursue true love and a deeper satisfaction, but the man-boy Roy Neary, who might be a fusion of Spielberg's mother and himself (the artist struggling to articulate a vision and find his medium and his aesthetic). No side doors for Spielberg here: in *Close Encounters*, he opens up the front entrance to his subconscious, like little Barry welcoming the visitors into his home, an uncomprehending yet curious child drawn to light, unafraid of blinding illumination or of being swept away into the unknown.

François Truffaut and Steven Spielberg during the filming of *Close Encounters of the Third Kind*, 1976—© Brigitte Lacombe

CLOSE ENCOUNTERS OF THE THIRD KIND DIARY

Bob Balaban

GILLETTE, WYOMING

May 17, 1976

FIRST DAY IN WYOMING. I'm exhausted and have a terrible headache. Finally got my bags, and am picked up at the tiny airport by a local driver from the movie. We start out for Gillette, which is two hours from the airport. He explains that we're going to the hotel, which is then an hour and a half from the location.

The countryside is beautiful. Rolling hills and lots of deer grazing. We drive for miles and miles without seeing another car. It's warm out. The driver explained that last week the temperature suddenly started dropping, and there were snowflurries. He says the weather is unpredictable here. He tells me that I'll be able to see Devil's Tower way in the distance if I look really hard. I stare and keep thinking I see it but the driver says I'm wrong. He says I'll know it when I see it.

I see a lot of signs pointing to Mount Rushmore and decide to try and get there on my day off. We keep driving; I try not to fall asleep. Finally, we near Gillette. Evidently I've missed the Tower. The green countryside turns to brown and trailer parks line the road. The driver explains that the construction industry can't catch up with the need for houses here, so most people live in trailers. We seem to be entering the heart of town, a main drag with lots of motels, bowling alleys and Denny's Restaurants. There are oil rigs everywhere. There's an IHOP and a Burger King, and no sidewalks. We pull into a two-story, slightly battered motel and I start unloading. Truffaut is staying here, but I don't see him. I imagine how strange it would be to run into François Truffaut at the ice machine.

The driver takes me to the location. We drive by more motels, bars and hamburger stands until we're in the countryside again. We pass through small canyons and rocky cliffs. The driver says I will be able to see the Tower as soon as we turn the corner. We make a sharp right and I can't believe what I see.

Devil's Tower looms ahead about fifteen miles in the distance, nine hundred feet of natural volcanic rock stretching straight up. It's a mammoth rectangle that stands out against the blue Wyoming sky as if it had been drawn on with a fine line marker. It's a very powerful sight.

I have been told that the studio wanted Spielberg to film all the Wyoming sequences at the Columbia ranch, a small patch of dirt and hills about a quarter of a mile down the road from the main studio buildings. I can see instantly why Steven chose Devil's Tower as a landing site for the Mothership, instead.

Further on, about ten miles from the Tower, hundreds of cars are creating a traffic jam. Trailers and lights are set up. Way in the distance, next to the camera, Steven is talking with Richard. I go over to say hello. I immediately notice that Richard looks very tired, and has a few days' growth. It doesn't dawn on me for a while that he has been made up to look this way. He is filming his arrival at Devil's Tower, and has spent the whole morning driving against traffic. It's been a difficult shot. Dreyfuss is very nearsighted. His character doesn't wear glasses, and Richard doesn't wear contact lenses. He has to take off his glasses as he drives the car, and he can't see a thing. He has been driving across mountainous terrain, trying to keep his car on the road. Steven tells me that Nick McLean, the camera operator, was stationed on the hood of the car filming, and he didn't realize how blind Richard really was without his glasses. At one point, he was so scared he insisted he be fastened more securely onto the hood of the car and that Richard drive more slowly.

Spielberg tells me to come by and watch a movie tonight. Richard and Spielberg have Winnebagos at the base of Devil's Tower so they don't have to get up early to drive to the location. They even have a cook out there. He's supposed to be very good, but he is having a hard time finding fresh vegetables. Truffaut was given one of the trailers too, but he didn't like staying in the woods, so he's back at the motel.

I go to wardrobe and try on my costumes. Nothing fits. They don't have thirty-six short. We all decide I will wear my own suits. The costume guy says it's a shame he didn't tell me to bring shoes.

· · · · ·

P.M.

Having dinner with François Truffaut and his translator tonight to speak about our scenes. I hope I'm too tired to be nervous. I leave my clothes in a wardrobe truck and get driven back to the motel around 4:30. I unpack some more and wait for a call from Truffaut.

At around six, Françoise Forget, the Columbia interpreter, calls and says Truffaut wants to meet me in the lobby. I hurry over. Truffaut looks very stern. I am nervous and very quiet. I suggest we have dinner at a restaurant about half a mile down the gravel road behind our motel. Truffaut says he hopes they don't have loud music in the restaurant. I seem to be able to understand him. As we walk, I try to: (a) think of anything to say, and (b) speak French. I can do neither. I do a lot of nodding, but it's pitch black out so Truffaut doesn't even see me.

We get to the restaurant. A country and western band is blaring. We take one look, turn around, and make the long walk back to the hotel again. All I can think of to say to Truffaut is that it's nice to meet him. I say this over and over again. I feel like a total idiot. We get to our hotel dining room. We're more relaxed, and dinner is actually fun. We make a lot of jokes about the steam table. All the food is "chicken-fried." It is impossible to translate chicken-fried steak into meaningful French.

Truffaut seems nice. He keeps asking for vegetables, and the sad little waitress keeps saying, "We have cottage cheese." I, of course, speak my normally fluent English to the waitress, who thinks I am French, too, and keeps repeating everything I say in English, in English. I tell Truffaut about my theatrical background. I tell him my grandfather was a Hollywood producer who discovered Esther Williams. Truffaut loves to talk about the old Hollywood studios. He thinks that New York writers were very snobbish about their attitude towards Hollywood, and says Hollywood studios have produced a lot of good movies. He says he is writing a book about actors, and he figures working for Spielberg is a great way to do some first-hand research.

After we finish ordering, I take out my script because I assume we're supposed to begin working. Truffaut looks very shocked and says we're not going to work until *after* dinner. I say I am very embarrassed. I feel like a social misfit. He laughs. I am starting to like him. After dinner we go back to the lobby to work a little. We read a scene together. Truffaut is a terrific actor and makes me smile when he speaks English. He says he would love to speak English as well as I speak French. This is the perfect thing to say to me. I don't believe him.

MAY 26

Truffaut and I go into the Devil's Tower Trading Post to buy some souvenirs …

We pack up the souvenirs and go outside. A group of small children have gathered to watch a helicopter carrying more equipment to the far side of the Tower. Truffaut notices some kids sitting on the curb of a gas station. He smiles and walks over to them and says hello. He looks so friendly that even though they don't understand what he is saying, he is instantly accepted as one of them. He sits down with the kids. One of them begins throwing stones to see if he can hit an old Mounds wrapper, and Truffaut joins him in the contest. They spend the afternoon sitting there, watching helicopters, and trying to hit the candy-wrapper with little pebbles. Truffaut tells me how much he loves to film small children. He says when you photograph a child you have a record of something that will never be duplicated. Everything children do is spontaneous; they are incapable of repetition.

He describes a scene from his new movie *Small Change* in which a little girl, left at home by her parents, runs to the window and shouts after them. The little girl he hired became suddenly shy when it was time to film the scene, and couldn't talk above a whisper. It was crucial to the scene to have her yelling out the window, and Truffaut didn't know what to do. He got an idea. He had the girl pick up a bullhorn from a chair, go to the window, and speak into it to her parents. The machine was turned all the way up, so no matter how softly the girl talked, her voice boomed louder. Later, Truffaut changed the profession of the girl's father, so that he could logically have a bullhorn in his house.

We both are eager to work on the Big Set in Mobile. I tell Truffaut I've heard that Steven is looking for little girls who are expert on rollerskates to play the extraterrestrials. (I have to dig up Forget to say the word for "rollerskates.") They will glide from the Ship on the rollerskates but will be shot from the ankles up, so they will appear to be floating. The Martian roller derby.

MOBILE, ALABAMA

JULY 12

François tells me today that before he began work on *Close Encounters* he called up Jeanne Moreau for advice on acting. She said he wouldn't have any problems, but that smiling would be difficult. Truffaut says her observation has been accurate. He also says that whenever he worked with Moreau she would develop a passionate hate for someone around the set: another actor, a wardrobe person, anyone. She would become fixated on this person. Days would become an endless series of avoided looks, delayed confrontations and hidden anger. Moreau explained that it did not have much to do with anything the other person was doing, it's just that when you're working for a long time in the same place, a scapegoat relieves the boredom and is good for concentration. Truffaut is telling me he is choosing a scapegoat himself. I tell him I am, too. We don't tell each other who they are; we'll see if we can guess later. I am very grateful I have Truffaut there to talk with all the time. I'm aware sometimes of other people looking enviously at us as we joke and laugh and tell each other great stories in French, and I feel lucky and a little possessive.

.   .   .   .   .

…. George Lucas, an old friend of Steven's, has come to observe, and he and Steven sit together watching a rehearsal. Julia Phillips comes by to say hello and the staff photographers have a field day. Lucas is editing a science fiction movie called *Star Wars*. Steven says that from what he's heard it should be very good.

.   .   .   .   .

.... This afternoon we were shooting Truffaut's reaction to a hovering UFO, touch it, and back away in awe. He rehearses it several times and then Steven shoots it. There is no dialogue, but it's hard to touch thin air and have a reaction of wonderment, happiness and awe at the same time. Steven has Truffaut do the scene over and over. I ask Truffaut if he minds a suggestion. He says of course not. I tell him that when he reaches up to touch the object he's got one hand on his hip and it looks too casual. I say that with his hand at his side he would probably look more reverential. Truffaut says "Aha!", and does the next take wonderfully, hand at his side. Spielberg yells "print," and I'm proud of myself. Truffaut asks me to keep watching him closely. He's afraid that his friends will laugh at him when they see the film, but I tell him not to worry.

JULY 24

Truffaut gives me another script to read. The author wants him to direct it, and he wants to send a very quick reply. The author has enclosed an extremely emotional letter with his script, describing the depth of his feelings for the material and the trials he has been going through trying to get it produced. I tell Truffaut that unfortunately the script is very much like another movie I've just seen, and is not very well written. I give Truffaut a brief synopsis of the plot. It's not something he would be interested in, but he admires the writer. He thinks hard for a moment; he wants to say something nice to the man. He gets an idea: he will write a letter explaining that the subject matter is too personal to be directed by anyone other than the author. He thanks me for reading it so quickly.

He goes to his desk and pulls out a book. It's the novel of his movie, *Small Change*. He writes a brief inscription on the inside cover and hands it to me. I can't stop smiling. I put the book away in my briefcase. For the rest of the day whenever I'm alone I take it out and look at the inscription:

> For Laughlin with my gratitude
> For Bob with my friendship,
> François Truffaut
> July 76

Bob Balaban during the filming of *Close Encounters of the Third Kind*, 1976—
© Brigitte Lacombe

INTRODUCTION TO

SMALL CHANGE: A FILM NOVEL

François Truffaut

F OR MANY YEARS I have been interested in true stories about childhood: newspaper clippings, stories by friends, my own memories, all feed my curiosity. *Small Change* was going to be the title of a collection of short stories, which I decided to abandon in order to turn it into a screenplay. To avoid making an episodic film, I have interwoven the action and characters of those stories and arrived at a form of collective chronicle.

The events of *Small Change* take place in Thiers during the last month of the school year, reaching their climax in August in a summer camp.

Small Change presents about ten youngsters, boys and girls, whose adventures illustrated—from the first feeding bottle to the first loving kiss—the different stages of passage from early childhood to adolescence.

The children, all of whom were newcomers to the movies, were recruited in Paris, Clermont-Ferrand, and Thiers. The parts of adults, parents and teachers, were given to little-known actors, as the true star of a film about children has to be childhood itself.

.　　.　　.　　.　　.

More than two hundred children's faces appear in the course of the story: a class of thirty-five students, another of twenty-five, a nursery with forty babies, and finally a summer camp with sixty boys and an equal number of girls.

As it is not easy to give a brief description of a collective film, I am going to summon to my aid three artists whom I admire.

.　　.　　.　　.　　.

Victor Hugo, in his *Art of Being a Grandfather*, Charles Trenet, in the course of two hundred and fifty popular songs of admirably even quality, and Ernst Lubitsch, indulgent and malicious at once—I see them as three poets who have succeeded in retaining the spirit of childhood.

> Children have a way of making me go crazy.
> I adore them and I am a fool.
>
> VICTOR HUGO

> Children are bored on Sundays,
> Sunday's children are bored.
>
> CHARLES TRENET

> An occasion to laugh is never to be despised.
>
> ERNST LUBITSCH

Those three quotations have been our guides, Suzanne's Schiffman's and mine, in the development of *Small Change*, in the choice of episodes and ways of dealing with them. It was a matter of making the audience laugh, not at the children but with them, nor at the expense of the adults either, but with them; thus we had to look for a delicate balance between gravity and humor.

. . . . .

Sylvie has misbehaved and cannot come to the restaurant; Richard lends his haircut money to two friends; Oscar refuses to talk and prefers to express himself by whistling; Bruno does not want to recite his lines "with the proper inflections"; Gregory falls out of a high window; Patrick falls in love with his buddy's mother; Julien is mistreated at home; Martine experiences her first kiss at summer camp. Obviously the web of *Small Change* is woven out of small events, but let us remember that nothing is "small" in the world of childhood.

Children see the world of adults as the world of impunity, the one in which everything is permitted. An adult can tell his friends with a smile how he happened to total his automobile by running it into a plane tree; on the other hand, a child who breaks a plate while drying the dishes thinks it has committed a crime, as it does not make a distinction between an accident and an offense.

Tossed about between their need for protection and their need for independence, children often have to endure adult caprices, and they have to defend themselves against them, to harden themselves. I stress the distinction: not to grow hard, but hard enough to stand it.

That is what Suzanne Schiffman and I want to express in *Small Change*, while obviously trying to avoid bombast and solemnity. Some of our episodes are funny, others serious, some are sheer fantasy, while others have been culled directly from grim media reports. Together they should animate the notion that childhood is often perilous but that it is also full of grace and that it has a thick skin. The child invents life; it runs into things, but at the same time it develops all its powers of resistance.

Finally, and this is obviously the raison d'être of the film, I never grow tired of making movies with children. Anything a child does on screen it seems to be doing for the first time, and that is what gives such a great value to film used to present young faces in the process of transformation.

FRANÇOIS TRUFFAUT
FEBRUARY 1976

TRANSLATED BY ANSELM HOLLO

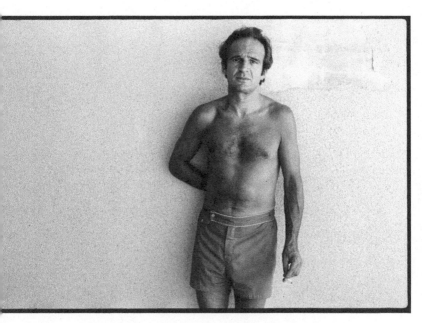

François Truffaut during the filming of *Close Encounters of the Third Kind*, 1976—
© Brigitte Lacombe

BY THE TIME I GET
TO PHOENIX

Thora Siemsen

"I grew up in the desert and have no merit in loving
it save in the solitude that preserves me from filth."

NICOLE BROSSARD, *MAUVE DESERT*

A s a child and then a teenager and then a young adult
in the outskirts of Phoenix, the desert never appeared
to me. From the window of the car, while driving south to
Tucson or north to Flagstaff, I saw nothing. It was only after
I'd been gone a long time and come back that I could begin
to perceive it. The usual trouble with hometowns is all the
trouble we get into in them, how youth obscures geography.
By the time we're old enough to remember what we see, it's
nothing new.

Would it be different had my view been of the sea? Romy
Hall, the protagonist of Rachel Kushner's 2018 novel *The Mars
Room*, lives in an expensive and storied coastal city, but because
she was born there she calls it Suckville. It is a place she looks
upon as a series of traps baited with temporary fixes for loneliness and privation. "What I eventually came to understand,"
she thinks, "was that I was immersed in beauty and barred
from seeing it."

I've seen the movies. Archie Mayo's 1936 film *The Petrified Forest* opens on the sight of tumbleweeds blowing down a road. Painted backdrops resemble the Painted Desert. The sign outside the service station reads LAST CHANCE FILL UP HERE. It's a family business on the edge of nowhere. A group of linemen are dining inside. Broadcasts about a killer on the loose are coming through the radio's whine. Bette Davis plays Gabrielle Maple, a young woman whose mixed signals sound to her suitor, a service station attendant called Boze, "like the hottest torch song that was ever sung." She's not much interested. The poetry of François Villon demands her attention. Her idea of small talk is asking a stranger, a writer named Alan Squier (played by Leslie Howard), who has just thumbed his way there, if he finds it cruel of her mother to have left her in Arizona for France. Shortly after meeting, Gabrielle and Alan climb up to the roof so she can show him her landscape paintings. She continues her pining for everything she still can't see from up there.

> ALAN: But don't you realize there are probably thousands of artists in France who are saying, if only I could get out to Arizona?
> GABRIELLE: I know. A lot of people go crazy about this desert when they see it. They seem to think it's full of mystery and haunted and all that.

Squier isn't so good at being casual himself. He hints at being suicidal early on in their acquaintance, telling Gabrielle of his itinerary, "I had a vague idea I'd like to see the Pacific Ocean… or perhaps drown in it, but that depends." On what?

On whether he can find something worth living and dying for by the time he gets there.

What's worse: being rudderless, or having a fixed but unlikely goal? Joshua Logan's 1956 film *Bus Stop*, featuring Davis's *All About Eve* co-star Marilyn Monroe, is another Arizona picture about chasing the mirage. Here, the desert is no longer in black and white but photographed in CinemaScope and Deluxe Color by cinematographer Milton Krasner. Monroe plays a saloon singer named Cherie, who says at the film's beginning, "If you don't have a direction, you just keep going around in circles." For most of the movie, she carries around a map as a reminder of her destination. Her goal is always out of reach, Phoenix as close to Hollywood as she'll get. She is an innocent who sees herself as wicked, spoiled too soon. Her new admirer, Beauregard "Bo" Decker (played by Don Murray), is a bully but innocent too. He is from a nowhere to which he'll return; Cherie's hometown gets flooded off the map. In the end, she loses her direction but finds a degree of acceptance by his side. "I guess I've been treated worse in my life," is how she eventually succumbs. Their bus heads off towards his ranch in Montana; it's her dreams that stop.

You could, if you'd like, synopsize *Bus Stop* and Martin Scorsese's *Alice Doesn't Live Here Anymore* the same way: a singer bound for California gets waylaid as a lounge act in Arizona before settling down with an infatuated rancher. In Scorsese's 1974 feature, Ellen Burstyn's Alice is on her way to Monterrey when she runs out of money in Phoenix. She is a new widow with her preteen son Tommy in tow. They live out of motel rooms that Alice rents for a song. Waitress is a bad word she eventually wraps her mouth around. Men in cowboy hats go around breaking things, most of all her trust. David (Kris Kristofferson), a regular at the diner job she takes, is the best of them. With David she can actually talk, as she does about her marriage to her late husband:

> ALICE: I got married and Donald wanted to live in his hometown.
> I wanted to go on singing. He said, "No wife of mine is going to sing in a saloon." I said, "Yes, master." I kind of liked that.
> DAVID: You liked it?
> ALICE: It was like, you know, my idea of a man: strong and dominating.

To better understand this kind of troublesome yearning, we can turn to its bard. On Joni Mitchell's "Down to You" from her album *Court and Spark*, released the same year as *Alice*, she sings: "Knocking for you, constant stranger / You're a brute, you're an angel." Who knows which one of his contrasting aspects will win out. And unknowability, while often diverting, turns out to be a mirage: violence is just bleak. But when you're in it, when your fear and desire are mixed up in illegible ways, *there isn't any other song* (Marilyn's best line in *Niagara*).

In Frank Pierson's 1976 remake of *A Star Is Born*, which the director co-wrote with Joan Didion and John Gregory Dunne, Kristofferson plays another Tucson rancher—*the* archetypal brute-angel—in a role initially offered to Elvis. As John Norman Howard, a burned-out rock star, Kristofferson courts disaster and Barbra Streisand's saloon singer Esther Hoffman with equal enthusiasm. She uneasily becomes a party to his chaos.

For their second "date," they take a helicopter to Tempe where he's playing a massive stadium show. (To pack the venue for filming the scene, the film's producers had to throw a real, all-day music festival with cheap tickets and big headliners including Peter Frampton and Santana; *The Arizona Republic* has claimed it was the largest concert in Arizona history at that time.) If you've seen any of the four versions of *A Star Is Born*, you know how this plays out. "Everywhere you go fighting breaks out and things get broken. Have you noticed that?", Hoffman asks him after the dust settles.

Time drying out in the Sonoran Desert does Howard good, as we see in a montage of the couple's newly wedded bliss. They begin building a home from nothing. Hoffman pulls up in a flatbed truck loaded with rustic furniture before the house's foundation is even laid. They roll around in the tall grasses kissing, possibly their brightest hour. Still, the rock star's infamy leaves him obsolete, uninsurable. And so he lives up to those low expectations. "I had my radio turned off for about a minute," he says of being usurped in listeners' affections by his old band, to say nothing of Hoffman's breakthrough success. *A Star Is Born* is the only one out of these movies where we see the woman's worldly dreams realized.

Polly Platt, production designer for the film, was responsible for the couple's home being an Arizona ranch and not a beach house on the California coast, as it had been in previous versions (Fredric March's Norman Maine suicides by walking into the Pacific Ocean in the 1937 original). In this case, the desert was haunted. Platt had lived in southern Arizona herself, and not only was the set fashioned after where she had previously lived as a newlywed, but the film's tragic car crash scene was filmed on the same stretch of land where Platt's first husband had fatally wrecked a sports car eight months into their marriage in 1959.

Among its mysteries: the desert, superficially inhospitable to life, has come to offer for many a chance at rebirth. Such is the hope of the protagonist Rose in Kate Braverman's novel *Lithium for Medea*, a very loose retelling of the myth: her Jason is a slumlord styled like a cowboy, her sacrifice is a cat named Picasso. Released in 1979, it was described by Didion as "jumpy, kinetic, and finally very powerful, a deeply felt piece of work by a very gifted young writer," one of those gifts being the ability to meaningfully describe youth. Rose is a 27-year-old addict in Los Angeles, which she experiences as a "city stretched on all sides, ripe with my intangible past. Not simply street corners but distinct places, invisible doors into other eras." When it is time to leave the city that has seen her brutalized, she gets in the car. Armed with a new, quivering sobriety, she drives and drives into the desert until nightfall. A bumper sticker advertising the Petrified Forest suggests a destination:

> I've got to keep going, cross the Arizona border... And north is the Grand Canyon, solved equation of windlash, water and time. And somewhere the great mountains where forests branch infinite fir and evergreens, alwaysgreens piercing granite, the spine, substantial and possible, possible.

Her eyes are on the road and she is alive, alone.

MY GUY

Hilton Als

F OR GOOD OR FOR ILL, Sam Shepard is the most objecti-
fied male writer of his generation. People who have little
interest in theater have found themselves drawn to it, and to
him, in part because of his looks, especially during the height
of his fame as a screen actor. (He has appeared in more than
forty movies and was nominated for an Oscar in 1984, for his
performance in *The Right Stuff.*)

Born Samuel Shepard Rogers VII in Fort Sheridan, Illinois,
in 1943, Shepard spent much of his childhood on a ramshackle
avocado ranch in Duarte, California. Loneliness permeated the
Shepards' home. Samuel VI, an Army pilot turned schoolteacher,
was an alcoholic and would disappear for days at a time. The
surrounding landscape—Route 66, the dusty "Main Street
of America," ran alongside Duarte—was not a comfort. Tall,
slightly snaggletoothed, and eagle-eyed, Shepard always looked
like America, or a movie version of America: one could easily
imagine him playing Tom Joad or Abraham Lincoln. His Western
drawl was an additional attraction. Joan Didion's essay about the
charisma of John Wayne could just as easily apply to Shepard:

> He had a sexual authority so strong that even a child could per-
> ceive it. And in a world we understood early to be characterized

by venality and doubt and paralyzing ambiguities, he suggested
another world, one which may or may not have existed ever but
in any case existed no more: a place where a man could move
free, could make his own code and live by it; a world in which, if
a man did what he had to do, he could one day take the girl and
go riding through the draw and find himself home free.

Shepard moved to New York in 1963 and roomed, for a time, with a friend from Duarte—Charles Mingus III, the son of the storied jazz musician. From Mingus, a mixed-race kid who painted, Shepard learned that the more straitlaced the woman the more she was attracted to difference. "Charles had this knack of picking up these amazingly straight women—stewardesses and secretaries," Shepard said, in Don Shewey's rich 1985 biography. "Charlie was always splattered with paint, and I didn't take too many baths back then. And there were cockroaches all over the place. But these women would show up in their secretarial gear."

Supporting himself as a security guard and a busboy, Shepard was encouraged to write plays by impresarios as diverse as Ellen Stewart, who established La MaMa, an experimental venue for new playwrights, in 1961, and Ralph Cook, who founded the Theatre Genesis, in 1964. They needed material, and the prolific Shepard soon needed as many stages as possible on which to present the voices he'd heard growing up—and the wound of rejection he'd experienced again and again in his own family.

Like many alcoholics, Shepard's father wasn't willing to share the stage, and, in a sense, Shepard's fifty-odd plays are a bid for his attention, albeit from a distance. As expressive as Shepard's characters are about their creator's interior life, they also stand guard between him and the hurting world. Many of Shepard's scripts—including *Buried Child* (1978), which won the Pulitzer Prize, *True West* (1980), and *A Lie of the Mind* (1985)—are about the adhesions that bruise even as they hold together the writer's boozy, self-deluding, and crippled families. But some brilliant early works, such as *La Turista* (1967), Shepard's first full-length play, *Cowboy Mouth* (1971), the first production of which starred Shepard and his sometime paramour Patti Smith, and the astounding *The Tooth of Crime* (1972), have a sharper, more intense focus, on couples and coupling. In these plays, the atmosphere is electric with disasters that seem to unfold in slow motion, or in the time it takes Shepard's characters to express their hatred, longing, or disappointment, much the way drunks express themselves—through repetition.

In *La Turista*, we meet an American couple, Salem and Kent, who are traveling in Latin America. The pair speak bad Spanish and complain about the locals. Both severely sunburned when we meet them, they talk about the pros and cons of different skin tones. In their jumble of specious theories, what Kent and Salem share is their whiteness, which is to say their preconceptions about how and when the world turns. The aging rock star Hoss and the musical upstart Crow, in *The Tooth of Crime*, are white, too. But, more important, they're male, and their masculinity informs all their actions. In the play's second act, the two men have a verbal showdown, monitored by a referee. The argument, ultimately, is about how the younger artist must devour the older one in order to feed his own work, his own myths. Crow says, of Hoss, "Can't get it together for all of his tryin'. Can't get it together for fear that he's dyin'. Fear that he's crackin' busted in two."

The 1983 play *Fool for Love* (in revival at the Samuel J. Friedman and conscientiously directed by Daniel Aukin) displays all the skill that Shepard developed when crafting his longer family plays but sacrifices none of the intensity and oddness of the earlier work. The play is not so much about coupling as about the deep impulses that keep people together even when they're apart. While writing *Fool for Love*, Shepard himself "busted in two," in order to talk about objectification from both a male and a female point of view.

To look at Judy Linn's 1971 photographs of Shepard (who was then married to the actress O-Lan Jones) with his lover Patti Smith, or to listen to Joni Mitchell's 1976 song "Coyote," which is ostensibly about the playwright—"There's no comprehending / Just how close to the bone and the skin and the eyes / And the lips you can get / And still feel so alone / And still feel related"—is to witness something rare in American masculinity: a man who found in himself something those female artists could *use*. Shepard wasn't averse to being taken over by a woman. (In a 1997 interview in *The Paris Review*, he said, "More than anything, falling in love causes a certain female thing in a man to manifest, oddly enough.") Through these powerful women and their creativity, he experienced the very opposite of Dad's disregard: validation and attention, the eyes of love that we all hope will help shape us.

Writing *Fool for Love*, during a time of emotional turmoil—Shepard's marriage to Jones was dissolving, and he was falling for another actress, Jessica Lange, with whom he would be involved for almost thirty years—made him jumpy and suspicious of his work. "The play came out of falling in love," he said, in *The Paris Review*. "It's such a dumbfounding experience. In one way you wouldn't trade it for the world. In another way it's absolute hell." The play, he added, baffled him. He felt close to his characters, the ex-lovers Eddie and May, but he didn't know how to guide them satisfactorily for the stage, how to express what needed expressing:

> I love the opening, in the sense that I couldn't get enough of this thing between Eddie and May, I just wanted that to go on and on and on. But I knew that was impossible.... I had mixed feelings about it when I finished. Part of me looks at *Fool for Love* and says, This is great, and part of me says, This is really corny. This is a quasirealistic melodrama. It's still not satisfying; I don't think the play really found itself.

But when does love find itself? Eddie (Sam Rockwell) loves May (Nina Arianda), but he's no good when it comes to love's realities, which include staying put until passion either deepens or withers into something else. He's always looking for the high of love: desire is his drug. And that addiction can be pretty wearing on a practical girl like May. When Shepard introduces us to Eddie and May, they're in their thirties, but their stop-and-start story began long before, when they were kids, really. Life has taught them a thing or two, not least how impossible their connection, or any intimacy, can be.

To escape Eddie's ambivalence, his need for attention, and his endless bullshit, May has moved to a dingy motel room on the edge of the Mojave Desert. She has just about caught her breath, started dating a nice guy named Martin (the sweet and stalwart Tom Pelphrey), and settled into a job as a restaurant cook, when Eddie shows up. He's not interested in May's urge to change her life; it doesn't benefit him in any way, and he's less of a person without her. The first words Eddie says are the words he thinks May wants to hear: "May, look. May? I'm not goin' anywhere. See, I'm right here. I'm not gone." May's heard all that before. Still, she clings to him—literally—wrapping her arms around his legs as he speaks. Eddie digs her dependence—until he doesn't. "Come on. You can't just sit around here like this," he says. "You want some tea? With lemon? Some Ovaltine?" May shakes her head. Outside, you can hear crickets singing in the night.

The dance of love and anger that Eddie and May are performing is choreographed; the furious partners know its steps. She knees him in the groin, and he falls to the floor. Recovering, he picks himself up and lays more charm over the hurt, like a kid holding a steak to a black eye. In jeans, boots, and a cowboy hat, Eddie is very confident when it comes to his charm: seduction is part of his lonesome-cowboy performance. Whether he's pacing around May's room or putting on his spurs to impress Martin, who shows up in the middle of this seventy-five-minute, Strindberg-like drama, he takes up a lot of psychic space.

Indeed, part of what May is fighting for is a little mental headroom. When she slams herself against a wall, she does so, in part, to set her incredulous brain straight: Did Eddie really say that? What does he want from her, now that he's sniffing around someone else? Eddie's other woman, whom May calls the Countess, hovers like a perfumed ghost over the couple's conversations. She's some sort of star—she was on the cover of a magazine, May tells us—and, although Eddie denies it, who else could own the huge black Mercedes-Benz that rolls up outside May's door about halfway through the story? She, for sure, doesn't know any women like that.

Even though May and Eddie are, for the most part, alone in her room, they're never really alone. Besides the Countess and Martin, there is someone else present: the Old Man (incredibly well played by Gordon Joseph Weiss). He may not be physically in the action, but psychically he's all over Eddie and May. For most of the play, he sits, in semi-darkness, downstage right, a short distance from May's bed and the red neon sign that flickers just outside her front door.

Fool for Love is a kind of existential boxing match, but the Old Man is no referee; he's grappling with his own problems and shadows. It turns out that Eddie and May are half siblings; the Old Man fathered them both, with different mothers, whom he abandoned. They are blood but also not blood. By the time they discovered this, it was too late. Love made them foolish, needy, bound by forces they couldn't explain:

> I was in love, see. I'd come home after school, after being with
> Eddie, and I was filled with this joy.... All I could think of was

> him…. And all he could think of was me. Isn't that right, Eddie?
> We couldn't take a breath without thinking of each other. We
> couldn't eat if we weren't together. We couldn't sleep. We got sick
> at night when we were apart. Violently sick. And my mother even
> took me to see a doctor. And Eddie's mother took him to see the
> same doctor but the doctor had no idea what was wrong with us.

Love also made them unsympathetic to their own mothers'
grief. May's need to escape Eddie is also a need to escape her
mother's devastation—"Her eyes looked like a funeral"—but
who ever achieves that?

Shepard adores May. You can feel him sitting back and wondering at her practical matter-of-factness; it makes him starry
with longing, with words. *Fool for Love* begins as the story of a
man's seduction and betrayal, but it ends up being dominated
by a woman's truth-telling. The play reminds me of another
Joan Didion remark: that, in the West, "men tend to shoot, get
shot, push off, move on. Women pass down stories."

Arianda and Rockwell pass down Shepard's story in unexpected ways that are informed by their lionhearted fearlessness
when it comes to failing. To understand Eddie and May is to
understand that it's nearly impossible to get those characters
"right"; as written, they keep drifting, losing ground, walking
away, or rushing toward emotions that Shepard treats like dunes
of beautiful shifting Mojave sand. The only way to nail the
doomed couple is to play them the way a jazz master plays a
tune: differently from day to day, from moment to moment. I
saw two performances of the play, and could have seen more,
in order to appreciate the nuances that Arianda and Rockwell

added or took away each time. At one performance, the energy was down, and Rockwell did everything he could to rev up the proceedings. Arianda, during the other show, created an atmosphere that explained, through movement and action, who May really was: a mother to the boy in Eddie—the only parent who could understand him. The actors did nothing for show, because they couldn't: for all its high drama, the script demands an incredible level of focus and concentration that isn't about "acting"—it's organic. As May packed a suitcase and walked through the door at the end of the play, it wasn't hard to imagine her meeting her literary predecessor out there in the dark world: the dogged Lena, in William Faulkner's *Light in August*. You remember Lena's great moment: she has just given birth to the child of her feckless lover, who immediately runs off. Staring after him, Lena tells herself, "Now I got to get up again."

THE NEW YORKER, OCTOBER 19, 2015

WILD TO THE WILD

Sam Shepard

THIS WAS IN THE DAYS when you could still mail-order wild baby animals from ads in the back of hunting and fishing magazines, like *Field and Stream*. You just sent away for them with your check or money order, and a month or so later they'd arrive, snarling and spitting in a wooden crate, down at the train depot. My friend Mitchell Chaney, who played slide trombone in our three-piece combo at high school, had collected almost every wild baby animal available at the time. (Nobody'd ever heard of an "endangered species.") I'd gone in with him on a couple of the cheaper ones, like the baby alligator and the baby armadillo, for instance. They were all kept at Mitchell's place, though, because we had too many dogs at ours and my dad was a firm believer in leaving the wild to the wild.

Evenings, when we'd rehearse our band over at Mitchell's, we'd go out in his backyard and make the rounds, checking all the cages, making sure the water and feed tanks were full, hosing out the messes they'd made (especially the spider monkey), and adding strands of coat-hanger wire to the mesh on the wolf pup's trapdoor. We couldn't find wire thick enough to keep him in. It would take him two or three days, but he'd eventually chew right through it, sometimes leaving a bloody tooth dangling behind. Then he'd end up wandering around on the railroad tracks that bordered Mitchell's backyard, killing chickens and rooting through the neighborhood garbage. We had a hell of a time catching him too, trying to bait him with raw hot dogs and then dragging him back with a tow chain borrowed from Mitchell's dad. He was getting to be a good size now—about sixty pounds and pure muscle. The Union Pacific ran a fruit train through town about six o'clock every evening, and we were both well aware of the deadline for getting our wolf out of its path.

Nat Henkins, our clarinet player, was not into the wild baby animal thing like me and Mitchell were. It just didn't interest him for some reason. In fact, the only thing that seemed to twirl Nat's ticket was forties big band music. The Dorsey Brothers and that ilk. He modeled himself after the young Benny Goodman, parting his hair straight down the middle and slicked back with pomade; he wore heavy black-rimmed glasses and kept his top button buttoned at all times. He also read sheet music fluently, which kept me and Mitchell somewhat in a state of awe, although privately we thought he was a dipshit. He was the only clarinet player in school, though, so we had to make do. Of the three of us, Nat looked the most out of place trying to pull a wolf pup off the railroad tracks. His body never looked fully committed to the task. Neither did his clothes. He would rest too long between pulls and spend a lot of time wiping the palms of his hands on his pants and staring vacantly down the tracks. His hands were extremely white and long-fingered, with milky, soft nails. The groans he made when he pulled on the chain were full of complaint rather than true effort, and this started to piss me and Mitchell off. We could sense Nat's halfhearted-ness and lack of urgency. Mitchell's voice was punctuated by gasps for air as he leaned against the weight of the baby wolf: "You understand, Nat, that the fruit train is gonna be blasting through here in about fifteen minutes? You understand that, don't you? We gotta get this wolf off the tracks!"

"It never blasts through," Nat said. "That's an exaggeration. They're not allowed to blast through towns. It's a law. They have to slow down when they see civilization. Besides, I don't see why you don't just turn him loose. Wolf's not gonna just stand here and let himself get smashed by a fruit train. He's not that stupid."

Mitchell stopped pulling and stood up straight, staring hard into Nat's lean face. "He's a wild animal, Nat. It's got nothing to do with 'stupid.' He's wild. He's never seen a train before in his life. He doesn't know about trains."

"Doesn't mean he's gonna let himself get creamed by one. He hears the noise and the whistle, he'll run. It's a natural instinct." Nat's levelheadedness only seemed to fire Mitchell's anger.

"I've got the feeling you could give a shit about the fate of our baby wolf, Nat."

"I'm just sick of wasting all this time when we could be practicing. Every time I come over, you guys are always messing around with these dumb animals. It takes us forever to get started."

"So you wanna just turn him loose and let him get hit by a train or a car or run off in the hills and die somewhere?"

"He's not gonna die in the hills. He's a wolf, for Christ's sake."

The pup just sat there with his hocks dug into the gravel, panting and drooling on the rail, his tongue darting in and out like a pink lizard. I dropped the chain and sat down on the cold rail beside the pup. The wolf's breath smelled like raw hot dogs and cottage cheese, which was exactly what we'd been feeding him. I stared into his yellow eyes and saw that he had no recognition of me in the way that my dogs did. He wasn't expecting anything from me, like a pat or a handout. He was in a world of his own. His head looked suddenly huge, like the close-ups of King on *Sergeant Preston of the Yukon*.

"What're we gonna do with this wolf, Mitchell, when he gets full-grown?" I asked, without taking my eyes off the pup. "Did you ever think of that?"

"We're gonna breed him. There's a huge market for hybrids." Nat snickered and shook his head hopelessly at the ground. He pulled a pressed handkerchief out of his back pocket and started cleaning his glasses, holding them up to the fading sky, then breathing little clouds of fog on the lenses and rubbing in rapid flurries like he'd seen older men do. Mature men. Like his father, maybe, or his uncle. I suddenly saw that the difference between me and Nat lay in some hidden, secret pattern that had nothing to do with who we thought we were. Patterns of belief and behavior that accrued to us imperceptibly through the men we were growing up with. Men we took to be legitimate and irrefutable. "We're gonna breed him to one of your sheep dogs," Mitchell continued, but it was directed more toward Nat, as some kind of vague challenge.

"Which one?" I said.

"Whichever one's in heat. You can have pick of the litter."

Nat kept rubbing his glasses and squinting down at them as he spoke. "When're you guys ever gonna have time to rehearse?

You'll be running a zoo here pretty soon. You gotta make up your minds what line of work you're gonna follow in this life. You wanna be musicians or wolf breeders?" It was this smugness about Nat that drew me and Mitchell into a tighter camaraderie. This "philosophical" tone of his: using "this life" as though it would put us in our place; as though "this life" was up ahead of us somewhere and had nothing to do with trains or wolves or the waning light. Mitchell hunkered down on the tracks beside me, with our stubborn wolf between us, as Nat continued his little sermon: "You guys don't seem to realize it takes work to make a band. Years of dedicated work. It's got to be the first thing on your list. We can't even get straight through 'Old Black Magic' without making mistakes."

"I hate 'Old Black Magic,' to tell you the truth," Mitchell said as he tossed a chunk of gravel at the iron rail. "Stupid lyrics. 'Those icy fingers up and down my spine. That same old witchcraft when your eyes meet mine.' What kinda corny horseshit is that?"

"We're not playing the lyrics," Nat said. "That's not the point. It doesn't matter what the lyrics are. We're playing the tune. You hate the Peggy Lee version, but I've been trying to tell you we aren't trying to imitate the Peggy Lee version."

"What are we trying to imitate, then?" I asked.

"It's not a question of imitation," Nat persisted. "It's more like laying a foundation. We can't just develop our own style out of thin air."

"Why not?" Mitchell said.

"Because that's not the way it happens!" Nat got more agitated with his handkerchief-rubbing. "We have to memorize the old standards. We gotta get those down so well we could do them in our sleep. 'Blue Moon,' 'Down by the Old Mill Stream'—stuff like that. Classics. Then we can start to innovate and develop our own sound. It's a slow evolution. That's how a band gets born."

"Well, I'm sick of that forties shit," Mitchell said as he grazed the rail with another chunk of gravel. The wolf pricked his ears at the high stinging sound, then rolled over on his side and kept up his rapid panting.

"I think we oughta try some improvising," I said. "What's the point of memorizing the standards if we're never gonna play 'em? We never play them at the sock hops."

"Because it gives us a background to build on. A foundation," Nat said. "We're not gonna play sock hops forever. Without the basics, we're just fishing in the dark. How do you think all the greats got started? Ellington, Count Basie, the Dorseys? You think they just started improvising wildly, hoping for the best?"

"We're a three-piece outfit, not a goddamn orchestra!" Mitchell exploded. "If you wanna do some classic stuff, then let's do something like 'Madagascar,' not 'Satin Doll' and 'Old Black Magic.' That's for the old farts."

"Who did 'Madagascar'?" Nat asked, genuinely mystified, and Mitchell turned to me and smiled. I don't know why he smiled, because I'd never heard of the tune either.

"Wilbur De Paris," Mitchell said, turning smugly back to Nat.

"Who the fuck's Wilbur De Paris?" I said, and Mitchell snapped his head toward me like I'd betrayed some deep pact between us.

"New Orleans," Mitchell said, trying to give it an esoteric drift. "My dad's got it in his collection. I'll play it for you when we get back to the house."

"I don't know," I said. "I like the Chicago guys myself. That's about all I can listen to anymore. Beats the stew outa Perry Como anyhow."

"Like who?" Nat said. "Like who from Chicago?"

"Like J.B. Lenoir, that's who," I said.

"What'd he do?"

"'Eisenhower Blues.'"

"'Eisenhower Blues'?"

"Yeah, 'Eisenhower Blues.'"

"That's obscure," Nat said. "You wanna be obscure, or do you wanna develop into a real band?"

"I wanna be a veterinarian!" I said. And that shut Nat up for the rest of the time. He got so depressed and silent he just wandered off away from us, with his glasses dangling from his left hand and his head drooped way down into his chest. His feet slipped going down the gravel bank of the tracks, and he picked himself up without even brushing off his slacks. Me and Mitchell never laughed at him though. We felt kind of bad for him in his disappointment, but we didn't call out to bring him back or try to make things better for him. It was best he faced the music on his own. We watched him walk away, back to Mitchell's yard, and go through the broken iron gate without trying to close it behind him. He never looked back at us. He just kept walking down the driveway and out onto the street. As he hit the sidewalk, the bluish streetlamps all came on at the same time, as though triggered by his footstep.

The six o'clock fruit train moaned in the distance, and the crossings were clanging through town, all the way out to Fish Canyon. The wolf pup jumped up and pricked his ears, then shook himself the way a horse does, where the shiver travels from the neck down the backbone and out through the tail. Not like a domestic dog, who shakes himself all in one piece. He stopped panting and stared in the direction of the oncoming train. He gave a little whine, then turned and loped off away from us down the track, dragging the chain behind him. Me and Mitchell just stood and watched him run off into the night. We never even called out to him. He didn't know his name anyhow.

5/2/89 (Scottsville, Virginia)

Acknowledgments

This volume would not have been possible without the guidance and trust of Wes Anderson, and the extraordinary help and partnership of Ben Adler.

The editor expresses his sincere thanks to: Hilton Als, Melissa Anderson, Andy Auton (Penguin Random House UK), Bob Balaban, Daniel Balderston (Borges Center, University of Pittsburgh), Jeremy Bernstein, *The London Review of Books*, Ronald Christ, K. Austin Collins, Roger Do Minh, Dennis Dollens, Imogen Forster, Nan Goldin, Haden Guest, Molly Haskell, Liz Helfgott (Criterion Collection), Sarah Henry and Sean Cocoran (Museum of the City of New York), Ruth Hoffmann and Georgina Dallas (Magnum Photos), Janet Johnson and Brigitte Lacombe, Jasmine Kennedy (Condé Nast), Deborah Nadoolman Landis and Natasha Rubin (David C. Copley Center for Costume Design, UCLA School of Theater, Film & Television), University of the Arts London, Emily Lyon, Matthew McPhillips and Dana Altman (Westwood Gallery), Sebastian Mekas, John Mhiripiri (Anthology Film Archives), Susan Morrison, John Peet, Octavia Peissel, Jeff Posternak, Brittany Rassbeharry, Tucker Smith, Serge Toubiana, Éva, Joséphine and Laura Truffaut, Kate Wolf.

Dedicated to Laura and Oliver.

In memory of dear friends Michelle Materre, Adrienne Mancia, and Shawn Regruto.

JAKE PERLIN
NEW YORK, 2023

Biographies

HILTON ALS is a staff writer for *The New Yorker*. He won the Pulitzer Prize for his criticism in 2017. His latest book is *My Pinup*.

EVE ARNOLD was born in Philadelphia, Pennsylvania to Russian immigrant parents. She began photographing in 1946, first became associated with Magnum Photos in 1951 and became a full member in 1957. She was based in the US during the 1950s but went to England in 1962; except for a six-year interval when she worked in the US and China, she lived in the UK for the rest of her life. In 1995, she was made fellow of the Royal Photographic Society and elected Master Photographer—the world's most prestigious photographic honor—by New York's International Center of Photography. She has had twelve books published. Arnold passed away in January of 2012.

BOB BALABAN is an American actor, director, producer, and writer. He has appeared in numerous films, including *Close Encounters of the Third Kind*, *Gosford Park*, *The Grand Budapest Hotel*, *Monuments Men*, and *Moonrise Kingdom*, and television shows, such as *Seinfeld*, *The West Wing*, and *Girls*. Balaban has been nominated for an Academy Award, a Golden Globe, and an Emmy Award. Outside of his work in entertainment, Balaban is also an advocate for social and political causes. He has been involved in various organizations, such as the American Civil Liberties Union and Amnesty International.

JEREMY BERNSTEIN is an American physicist, writer, and educator. In addition to his work in physics, Bernstein is also a prolific writer and contributor to *The New Yorker*. He has written more than a dozen books on science and technology, as well as several books on politics and history. His books on science have covered a wide range of topics, including nuclear weapons, particle physics, and the history of science.

JORGE LUIS BORGES was an Argentine writer, poet, and essayist born in 1899. His works often blend elements of fantasy, philosophy, and existentialism, and explore themes such as identity, time, and memory. Some of his most famous works include *Ficciones*, *The Aleph*, and *Labyrinths*. Borges died on June 14, 1986, in Geneva, Switzerland at the age of eighty-six.

DURGA CHEW-BOSE is a writer and editor living in Montreal. She is the author of *Too Much and Not the Mood*, a collection of essays published by Farrar, Straus and Giroux in 2017. Her work has appeared in *Artforum*, *Vanity Fair*, *The New York Times Magazine*, *Aperture*, and *Harper's Bazaar*. She's written catalogue essays on a variety of artists including Agnes Martin, Ann Craven, Marcelo Gomes, and Wolfgang Tillmans. She's currently working on her first film.

K. AUSTIN COLLINS is a former film critic for *Rolling Stone* and a programmer for the New York Film Festival. He was formerly the film critic for *Vanity Fair* and *The Ringer*. He writes crosswords for *The New Yorker* and *The New York Times*. He lives in Brooklyn.

BOSLEY CROWTHER was a film critic of great influence for *The New York Times* for twenty-seven years, writing over two hundred pieces a year. He was a fierce opponent of censorship, McCarthyism, and the blacklist, and wrote multiple books and collections of writings including *The Lion's Share: The Story of an Entertainment Empire* and *Hollywood Rajah: The Life and Times of Louis B. Mayer.* Crowther passed away in 1981.

BRUCE DAVIDSON was born in Oak Park, Illinois, studied at the Rochester Institute of Technology and Yale University, worked as a freelance photographer for *Life* magazine and in 1958 became a full member of Magnum. From 1958 to 1961 he created such seminal bodies of work as East 110th Street, Brooklyn Gang, and Freedom Riders. He received a Guggenheim Fellowship in 1962 and created a profound documentation of the civil rights movement in America. In 1963, The Museum of Modern Art in New York presented his early work in a solo show. Classic bodies of work from his fifty-year career have been extensively published in monographs and are included in many major public and private fine art collections around the world. Bruce Davidson lives in New York City.

ELLIOTT ERWITT was born in Paris in 1928 to Russian parents. Erwitt spent his childhood in Milan, then emigrated to the US, via France, with his family in 1939. He attended Los Angeles City College, and in 1951 he was drafted for military service and undertook various photographic duties while serving in a unit of the Army Signal Corps. Erwitt joined Magnum Photos in 1953 and worked as a freelance photographer for *Collier's*, *Look*, and

Life. In addition to numerous legendary books of photography, Erwitt made the great film *Beauty Knows No Pain* (1972).

MOLLY HASKELL is a critic and author whose books include *From Reverence to Rape: The Treatment of Women in the Movies*; *Love and Other Infectious Diseases*; *Frankly, My Dear: Gone with the Wind Revisited*; and *Steven Spielberg: A Life in Films*. She won the 2017 career achievement award from the New York Film Critics Circle.

KENT JONES is a filmmaker and writer. His films include the 2010 documentary, *A Letter to Elia*, co-directed with Martin Scorsese, and *Hitchcock/Truffaut*. He made his fiction debut with the critically acclaimed *Diane*. He is the author of several books of criticism, and he served as Director of the New York Film Festival from 2013 to 2019. He is currently in pre-production on his next film, *My Ship*, based on his own script.

PAULINE KAEL wrote for *The New Yorker* from 1967 until her retirement, in 1991. She was the author of thirteen books, including *I Lost It at the Movies*, *Kiss Kiss Bang Bang*, *Deeper into Movies* (which won the 1974 National Book Award), and *5001 Nights at the Movies*. In 2011, her film criticism was anthologized in the Library of America.

ELIA KAZAN was born in Constantinople (Istanbul), co-founded The Actors Studio, and directed stage productions of *Death of a Salesman* and *Cat on a Hot Tin Roof*; his films include *A Streetcar Named Desire*, *On the Waterfront*, *East of Eden* and *Splendor in the Grass*. He is the author of *The Arrangement*, *America America*, and *The Assassins*. Kazan passed away in 2003.

MICHAEL KORESKY is the Editorial Director at The Museum of the Moving Image; co-founder and editor of the online film magazine *Reverse Shot*, a publication of MoMI; the author of *Films of Endearment* (Hanover Square Press, 2021) and *Terence Davies* (University of Illinois Press, 2014); a longtime contributor to the Criterion Collection and *Film Comment*; and the programmer of the series *Queersighted* for the Criterion Channel. He has taught on the history of American queer cinema at NYU and the New School.

STANLEY KUBRICK was an American film director, producer, screenwriter, and photographer. He was born on July 26, 1928, in New York City and passed away on March 7, 1999. Kubrick started his career as a photographer, and his early work was published in *Look* magazine. He went on to direct numerous masterpieces, including *Dr. Strangelove or: How I Learned to Stop Worrying and Love the Bomb* (1964), *2001: A Space Odyssey* (1968), *A Clockwork Orange* (1971), and *Eyes Wide Shut* (1999).

BRIGITTE LACOMBE is a French photographer known for her influential and revelatory portraiture. For four decades she has created iconic and intimate photographs of many of the world's most celebrated artists, actors, politicians, and intellectuals. She is currently at work on a visual memoir. As a special visiting photographer, Lacombe has worked behind the scenes on many film sets starting with Alan Pakula's *All the President's Men* and *Fellini's Casanova* both in 1975, and Steven Spielberg's *Close Encounters of the Third Kind* in 1976. Since then she has documented the films of Martin Scorsese, Alejandro González Iñárritu, Lynne Ramsay, Spike Jonze, Bennett Miller, Sofia

Coppola, Wes Anderson, Quentin Tarantino, Michael Haneke, Mike Nichols, among many others. Lacombe's many advertising campaigns include work for Dior, Chanel, Issey Miyake, Prada, Armani, Hermes, and Lancôme. She lives in New York City.

ANDY LOGAN was the first female Talk of the Town reporter for *The New Yorker*. Over the half-century-plus that she worked there, she contributed hundreds of thousands of words: Talk pieces, Profiles, That Was New York, Letters from Nuremberg (her husband, Charles Lyon, was deputy chief counsel at the Nuremberg war-crimes trials), the Christmas toy list and, most famously, the Around City Hall column.

JONAS MEKAS was a filmmaker and co-founder of the influential New York-based film journal *Film Culture* with his brother Adolfas. Mekas was a crucial figure in the New York film and arts community and longtime contributor to *The Village Voice*. As a filmmaker, his landmark works include *Walden* (1969) and *Lost, Lost, Lost* (1976). He is a co-founder of the New American Cinema Group and Anthology Film Archives in New York. Mekas passed away on January 23, 2019, at the age of ninety-six.

INGE MORATH was born in Graz, Austria, in 1923, and joined Magnum Photos in 1953. Morath traveled extensively in Europe, North Africa, and the Middle East. Her special interest in the arts found expression in photographic essays published by a number of leading magazines. After her marriage to playwright Arthur Miller in 1962, Morath settled in New York and Connecticut. Morath died in New York City on January 30, 2002.

LILLIAN ROSS was a staff writer at *The New Yorker* from 1945 until her death at age ninety-nine in 2017. Her classic book, *Picture*, about the making of the 1951 film *The Red Badge of Courage*, is generally acknowledged to be the first time a long factual story was written in a form resembling a novel. Her piece "Wes Anderson in Hamilton Heights," about the making of *The Royal Tenenbaums*, appeared in the May 13, 2001 issue of *The New Yorker*.

NICOLAS SAADA is a French film director, screenwriter, and producer. He began his career in the film industry as a critic and journalist for various French publications including *Cahiers du Cinéma*, and ran a radio program about soundtracks, *Nova fait son cinéma*. He later transitioned to filmmaking. He has received numerous awards and nominations for his work in film and television, including a César Award nomination for his first short film *Les Parallèles* in 2004, and Best First Feature Film for *Espion(s)* in 2009. His second feature *Taj Mahal* was selected in 2015 at the Telluride and Venice film festivals. He also directed the mini series *Thanksgiving* in 2019 for Arté.

ROY SCHATT was an American photographer, best known for his portraits of celebrities and artists. Schatt opened his own studio in New York City in the 1940s and quickly established himself as a leading portrait photographer. His subjects included many famous artists and celebrities of the time, such as Marilyn Monroe, James Dean, Marlon Brando, and Tennessee Williams.

MATT ZOLLER SEITZ is the Editor-at-Large of RogerEbert.com, a staff writer for *New York* magazine and *Vulture*, a finalist for the Pulitzer Prize in criticism, and the creator of video essays on film history and style for The Museum of the Moving Image, *Vulture*, and *Salon*. His books on film and TV include *The Sopranos Sessions*, *Mad Men Carousel*, *The Oliver Stone Experience*, *Guillermo del Toro's The Devil's Backbone*, and *The Wes Anderson Collection* series (five volumes and counting).

SAM SHEPARD was the Pulitzer Prize-winning author of more than fifty-five plays and three story collections. As an actor, he appeared in more than sixty films and received an Oscar nomination for *The Right Stuff*. He was a member of the American Academy of Arts and Letters, received the Gold Medal for Drama from the Academy, and was inducted into the Theater Hall of Fame. He died in 2017.

THORA SIEMSEN is a writer living in Colorado.

GEORGES SIMENON was born in 1903 in Liège, Belgium. He wrote over two hundred books of fiction and memoirs, the majority about Inspector Maigret. His novels have been adapted dozens of times for film and television, including *The Bottom of the Bottle*, one of four novels Simenon wrote while living in Arizona.

IMOGEN SARA SMITH is the author of *In Lonely Places: Film Noir Beyond the City*, and *Buster Keaton: The Persistence of Comedy*. Her writing has appeared in *Sight & Sound*, *Film Comment*, the Criterion Collection, and many other venues.

DENNIS STOCK was born in 1928 in New York City. At the age of seventeen, he left home to join the United States Navy. In 1947, he became an apprentice to *Life* magazine photographer Gjon Mili and joined Magnum in 1951. Stock managed to evoke the spirit of America through his memorable and iconic portraits of Hollywood stars, most notably James Dean.

GINA TELAROLI is a filmmaker, writer, archivist, and programmer. She was raised in Cleveland, Ohio, and lives in New York City.

SERGE TOUBIANA is a film writer and producer. He was Editor-in-Chief of *Cahiers du Cinéma* between 1981 and 1991. In addition to his work as a film critic and journalist, Toubiana has also produced several films. He co-produced the acclaimed 1991 film *Van Gogh*, directed by Maurice Pialat. Toubiana has written several books on film and filmmakers, including biographies of François Truffaut, Woody Allen, and Roman Polanski. He is also a member of the board of directors of the Cinémathèque Française, the prestigious film archive and museum in Paris.

FRANÇOIS TRUFFAUT was born in Paris in 1932. He wrote film criticism that helped redefine the careers of popular Hollywood filmmakers as major artists. He wrote and directed many masterpieces including *The 400 Blows*, *The Soft Skin*, *The Wild Child*, *Small Change*, *The Story of Adele H.*, and *The Green Room*. He passed away at age fifty-four, and his contributions are immeasurable.

Rights and Permissions

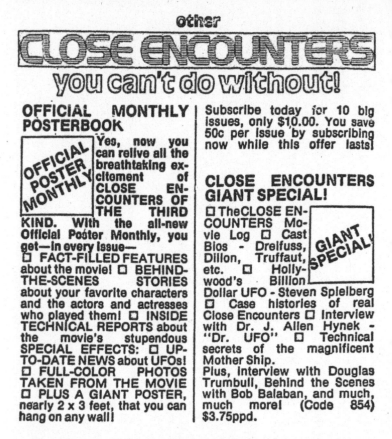